HOW TO
MACHINE
SEW

HOW TO
MACHINE
SEW

TECHNIQUES AND PROJECTS
FOR THE COMPLETE BEGINNER

SUSIE JOHNS

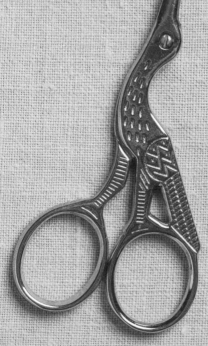

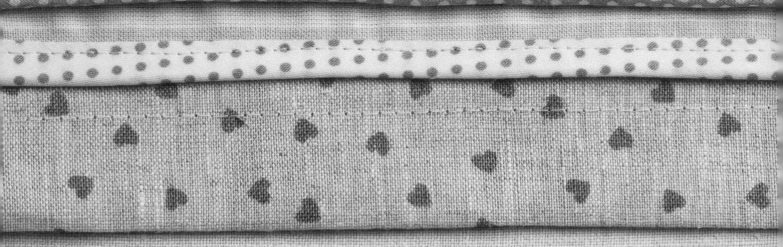

First published 2015 by
Guild of Master Craftsman Publications Ltd.
Castle Place, 166 High Street, Lewes,
East Sussex BN7 1XU

Text, designs and templates © Susie Johns, 2015
Copyright in the Work © GMC Publications Ltd, 2015

ISBN 978 1 86108 701 0

All rights reserved

The right of Susie Johns to be identified as the author of this work has
been asserted in accordance with the Copyright, Designs and Patents
Act 1988, sections 77 and 78.

No part of this publication may be reproduced, stored in a retrieval
system or transmitted in any form or by any means without the prior
permission of the publisher and copyright owner.

This book is sold subject to the condition that all designs are copyright
and are not for commercial reproduction without the permission of the
designer and copyright owner.

Whilst every effort has been made to obtain
permission from the copyright holders for
all material used in this book, the publishers
will be pleased to hear from anyone who
has not been appropriately acknowledged
and to make the correction in future reprints.

The publishers and author can accept no legal responsibility for any
consequences arising from the application of information, advice or
instructions given in this publication.

A catalogue record for this book is available from the British Library.

PUBLISHER Jonathan Bailey
PRODUCTION MANAGER Jim Bulley
SENIOR PROJECT EDITOR Sara Harper
EDITOR Kim Davies
MANAGING ART EDITOR Gilda Pacitti
DESIGNER Rebecca Mothersole
ILLUSTRATIONS Sarah Skeate
PHOTOGRAPHERS Rebecca Mothersole and Andrew Perris

Colour origination by GMC Reprographics
Printed and bound in China

CONTENTS

INTRODUCTION

To get the most from this book, you need only the most basic equipment and skills. If you have never used a sewing machine before, the techniques and projects will guide you through the basic processes: first learn a new technique, then try it out by making something useful or decorative – or both – for your home.

Creating things with fabric and thread not only gives you a great sense of achievement, it means that you can customize them with your own choice of fabrics and trimmings, and tailor them to suit your home and your lifestyle.

Fabric is a wonderful way to add colour, texture and interest to your home. Follow this simple course from beginning to end or, if you already have some sewing experience, use some of the chapters as a revision guide and others to build on your existing skills. Machine sewing is fun, creative and a lot easier than you might think.

GET ORGANIZED

This book, divided into sections, helps you to build your knowledge and confidence, providing you with a straightforward introduction to machine sewing – a skill that, until now, you might have thought was too difficult or perhaps too technical to attempt. Each section comprises a technique, carefully written and laid out in a way that is designed to help build your skills. To practise each technique, you'll find a project, once again broken down into clear step-by-step stages that help to simplify the processes involved. For example, after introducing the technique of binding and piping, there is an oven glove to make that uses both binding and piping. So, you can practise the techniques and end up with something practical and useful.

When trying a new technique for the first time, read through the instructions very carefully, then gather together all the materials and tools you will need to complete the project; being organized makes such a difference.

This is essentially a book for beginners. It outlines basic techniques, enough to get you stitching with confidence and making a range of items for your home. There are other – often more complicated – methods for, say, sewing seams, hemming, or fitting zippers and you can find out about these from other sources, once you have mastered the basics.

In the meantime, enjoy exploring and learning, developing skills and making the most of your sewing machine.

Susie

BEFORE
YOU START

CHOOSING AND USING A SEWING MACHINE

If you are new to sewing, a basic all-purpose machine is all you need. These days, however, it is more difficult to find a simple machine as many models are computerized and offer a dazzling array of stitches and sophisticated applications.

Get to know your machine before you begin sewing. Your machine may differ from the one shown here; if so, compare this diagram to the information given in your users' manual.

1 SPOOL PIN

This holds the spool of thread in place so that it doesn't move, and allows the thread to unravel without tangling as you stitch.

2 STITCH SELECTOR

This can be a dial or a lever or, on modern computerized machines, a touch pad.

3 THREAD GUIDES

These are wires or hooks that guide the thread from the spool to the needle.

Tip It is a good idea to choose a well-known brand of sewing machine so that parts are readily available if and when a repair is needed.

4 TAKE-UP LEVER

This pulls the thread off the spool – just enough to complete each stitch.

5 UPPER TENSION CONTROL

This adjusts tension for different thickness of fabric: the higher the number, the tighter the tension.

6 STITCH-WIDTH CONTROL

This controls the distance the needle moves from side to side. Most can be set to a maximum width of ¼in (5–6mm).

7 STITCH-LENGTH CONTROL

This determines the distance the feed dogs move the fabric along between each insertion of the needle.

8 REVERSE BUTTON

This can be also be a lever, or switch, and reverses the direction of stitching and is used to backstitch at the beginning and end of a row of stitching.

9 NEEDLE CLAMP

This is unscrewed when you want to remove and change the needle.

10 NEEDLE

The shank is inserted into the machine and has one flat side and one rounded side for proper positioning.

11 FEED DOGS

These are saw-shaped teeth that move the fabric as you stitch. The position of the feed dogs can be lowered; this is usually done when you are mending or embroidering, when you need to control the direction of the fabric.

12 THE PRESSER FOOT

This holds the fabric firmly against the feed dogs.

13 BOBBIN CASE

A bobbin (see page 15) is a small spool that is wound with thread and fits into a bobbin case below the throat plate. The bobbin is either dropped into the case or the case is removed and the bobbin inserted.

14 THROAT PLATE

Also known as the needle plate, this sits over the feed dogs. You will find parallel lines on the throat plate to use as guides for various widths of seam allowance.

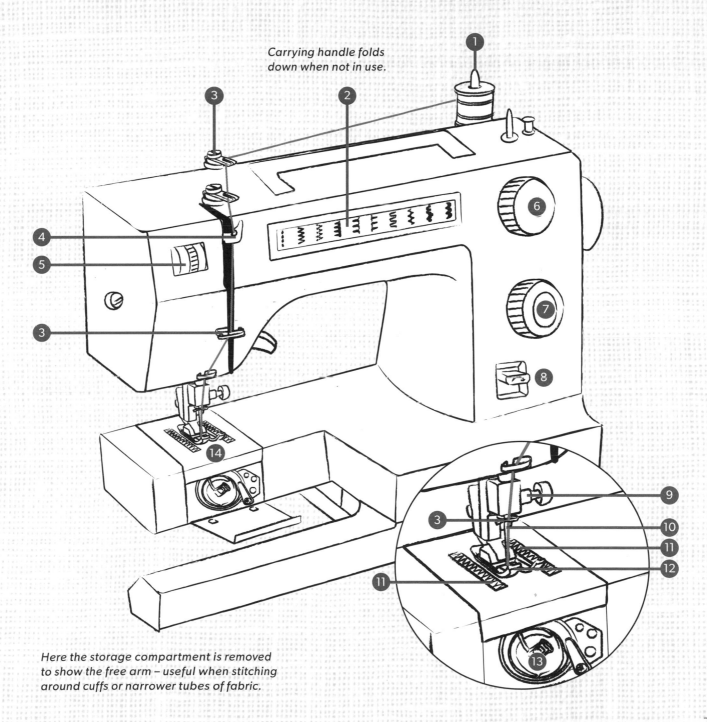

Carrying handle folds down when not in use.

Here the storage compartment is removed to show the free arm – useful when stitching around cuffs or narrower tubes of fabric.

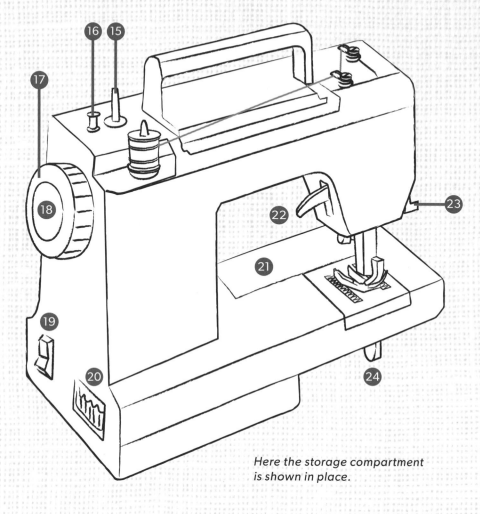

Here the storage compartment is shown in place.

18 CLUTCH WHEEL

This stops the needle moving while the motor is running and is engaged when the bobbin is being wound with thread.

19 POWER SWITCH

Turn this on to activate the machine.

20 POWER SOCKET

The power cord, which is attached to the foot pedal, plugs in to this socket.

21 STORAGE COMPARTMENT

There is often a removable storage compartment in the bed of the machine, to store spare needles, bobbins and other small items. When you remove this, the bed of the machine becomes narrower, allowing you to stitch around tubular pieces such as cuffs.

22 PRESSER-FOOT LEVER

This raises and lowers the presser foot. The presser-foot clamp can be unscrewed to remove the presser foot.

23 THREAD CUTTER

This consists of a small blade with a guard.

24 FEED DOG LEVER

Use this to raise and lower the feed dogs.

15 BOBBIN WINDER SPOOL

This mechanism enables you to load thread on to the bobbin so that it is smoothly and evenly wound.

16 BOBBIN WINDER STOP

This prevents the bobbin being over-wound with thread.

17 BALANCE WHEEL

Otherwise known as the flywheel, or hand wheel, this drives the needle up and down. You can turn the wheel by hand to raise and lower the needle at the beginning or end of a line of stitching.

SEWING MACHINE ACCESSORIES

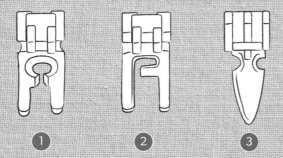

OTHER ACCESSORIES

Bobbins 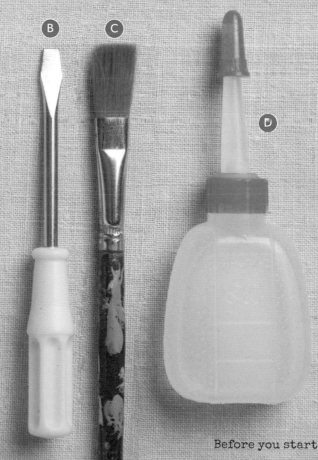 are loaded with thread: make sure you use the right type of bobbin for your machine.

Most machines come equipped with a small, flathead **screwdriver** B so you can unscrew the throat plate for cleaning or access the light bulb housing to change the bulb. A **brush** C is useful to clean fluff, lint and snippets of thread from the bobbin compartment, as is an **oil bottle** D to hold sewing machine oil for lubricating the various parts of the machine.

SEWING MACHINE FEET

The machine foot is interchangeable and most sewing machines come with a range of different feet. Here are a few of the most common and useful ones: all-purpose, embroidery and zipper.

1 The **all-purpose foot**, as the name suggests, can be used for all kinds of applications and on various fabrics.

2 An **embroidery foot** can be used for appliqué and embroidery: it is often made from transparent plastic so you can see the work underneath and it has a wide groove on the underside to glide over bumps and thick areas of stitching.

3 A **zipper foot** is used to stitch zippers and piping. It can be fitted on either side of the needle and allows you to stitch close to the edge of the teeth on a zipper.

HOW A SEWING MACHINE WORKS

The instruction manual for your machine will provide detailed instructions but most machines follow the same basic principle. The reel of thread (A) sits on top of the machine and the end of the thread is fed via a series of levers, channels and hooks (B) through the tension mechanism and finally down to the needle (C), where it is threaded through the eye.

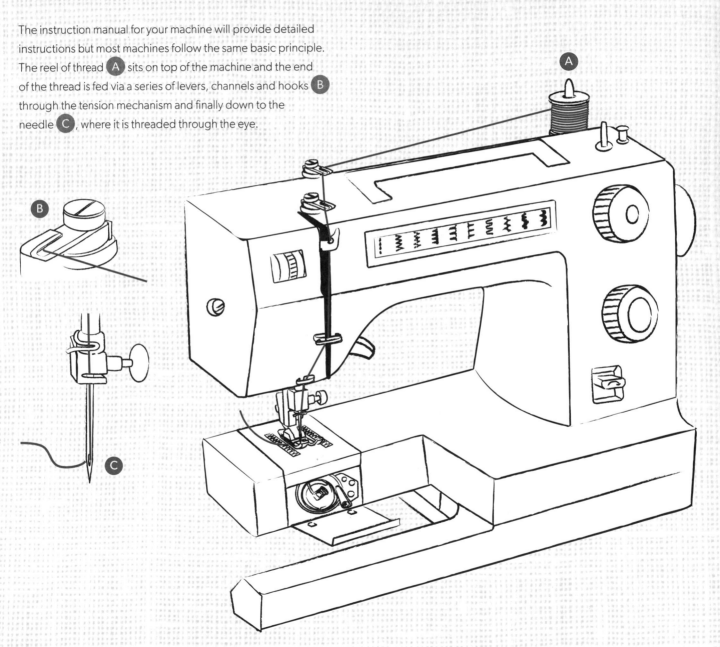

A second thread 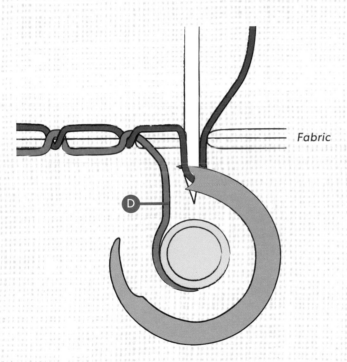 D, wound on to a bobbin, sits in a small compartment under the base plate, below the needle. When the machine is running, the needle dips down through the fabric into a hole in the plate and picks up a loop of thread from the bobbin, creating an interlocking stitch on both sides of the fabric.

Fabric

D

Tip For clarity, the top thread and the bobbin thread are shown here in different colours but you would usually use matching threads.

WINDING AND LOADING THE BOBBIN

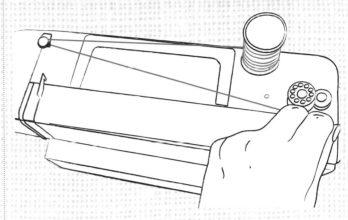

1 Push the end of the thread through the hole in the top of the bobbin (if it has one), from underneath, so that it sticks out of the top. Place the bobbin on the bobbin winder and hold the thread end; feed the thread that leads to the spool around the thread guide, according to your users' manual. Engage the bobbin winder by pushing it towards the bobbin winder stop, if necessary. (You may have to disengage the needle by pulling or pressing the clutch wheel, depending on the type of machine you have.) Wind the bobbin until it is full, then cut the thread.

2 Hold the bobbin case and insert the bobbin. Pull the thread into the slot of the case, then pull the thread to the left under the tension spring until it enters into the delivery eye.

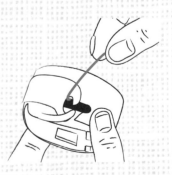

HOW TO THREAD YOUR MACHINE

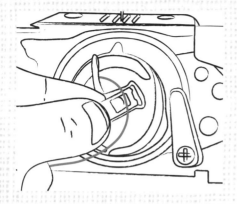

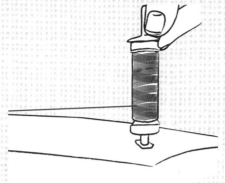

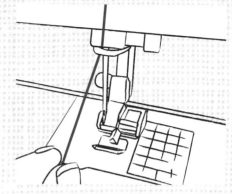

1 Insert the bobbin case into the compartment beneath the throat plate and click into place.

2 Put the spool of thread in place on top of the machine and place the spool holder or cap in position to secure the spool.

3 Pass the thread through the thread guides, down through the machine's tension mechanism.

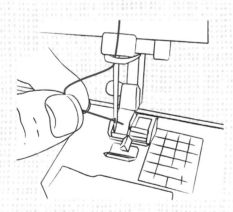

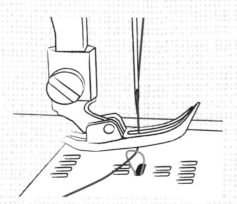

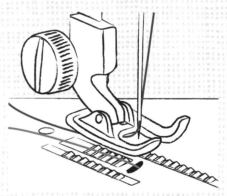

4 Lift the presser foot and turn the balance wheel to raise the needle. Pass the end of the thread through the eye of the needle. Some sewing machines include a needle threader mechanism to make this easier.

5 Hold the end of the bobbin thread and turn the balance wheel towards you so that the needle goes down and up again, picking up a loop of bobbin thread.

6 Let go of the end of the bobbin thread and pull on the top thread to pull out the loop of bobbin thread. Pass the two thread ends towards the back, behind the needle, ready to start stitching.

CHECKING YOUR TENSION

Test the stitch tension by sewing a line of stitching on a small swatch of fabric.

1 Cut two small pieces from the fabric you will be using. Set the tension on your machine to 4. Place one piece of fabric on top of the other and machine a line of stitching diagonally through them (along the bias of the fabric).

2 Now check the appearance of the stitching. If the tension is correct, the stitches interlock in the middle of the two layers and the lines of stitching will look the same on both sides.

Correct tension – the stitches interlock evenly,

Incorrect tension (1): if the top stitches appear too loose, the top tension needs to be tightened – so turn the tension dial to a higher number.

Incorrect tension (2): if the stitches on the underside appear loose, adjust the tension dial to a lower number.

MACHINE MAINTENANCE

- With use, your machine can collect dust, lint and small pieces of thread. Clean your machine regularly – ideally, after each project. Leaving it too long can slow down or even jam the inner workings of your machine.

- Before you start, make sure your machine is unplugged. Remove the sewing machine needle and the presser foot. Brush out underneath the presser foot, the feed dogs, the bobbin area, and every other nook and cranny that attracts dust. If your machine doesn't come with a brush, a small but firm-bristled paintbrush will do the job.

- Refer to your sewing machine manual for a diagram that shows you where to oil your machine. Put a drop or two on each marked spot. When you've finished, turn the hand wheel to make sure the oil is well distributed.

- Wipe the exterior of the machine with a soft, clean cloth. Replace the presser foot and the needle.

- Before you start a new project, thread the machine and sew a few rows of stitches on a scrap of fabric to make sure any excess oil comes off on the scrap, and not your project.

- Keep your machine covered when not in use.

BASIC TOOLS AND EQUIPMENT

❶ MACHINE NEEDLES

The manual for your sewing machine should include a guide to choosing and using needles. For most projects, a **multipurpose** or **universal needle**, size 12/80, will do the job. Replace the needle in your machine frequently, as sewing machine needles do not last very long: they become bent or rough and this will cause missed stitches, snags and tangles.

Different fabric weights will require different needle sizes. The table below provides a general guide.

SEWING MACHINE NEEDLE SIZES

US	UK
8	60
10	70
11	75
12	80
14	90
16	100
18	110
20	120

❷ NEEDLE THREADER

Threading a needle can sometimes be frustrating, so keep a needle threader in your work box. This tiny gadget has a wire loop that you push through the eye of the needle; you then pass the end of the thread through the wire loop, then withdraw the loop from the needle, pulling the thread through the eye at the same time.

❸ HAND-SEWING NEEDLES

Even though you are machine sewing, you will need some hand-sewing needles for various tasks. Buy a pack of assorted needles and choose a needle that is suitable for the thickness of the fabric and the thread: the smaller the number, the finer the needle.

❹ SCISSORS

Use a small pair of **sharp scissors** with pointed blades Ⓐ for snipping threads. For cutting fabric, make sure you have good-quality **dressmaking shears** Ⓑ and keep them only for cutting fabric, not paper or other materials. Keep a pair of **all-purpose scissors** Ⓒ for cutting paper and card when making templates. **Pinking shears** Ⓓ, with zigzag blades, are useful for cutting fabrics that have a tendency to fray.

❺ STITCH RIPPER

Useful if you need to unpick a seam: it has a hooked end containing a small blade that will cut threads between fabric layers.

SHARPENING SCISSORS

Scissors should be kept sharp. Blunt scissors will make cutting fabric difficult and inaccurate. Invest in a good pair of dressmaking scissors – sometimes referred to as shears – and have them sharpened professionally on an annual basis; many shops that sell sewing machines offer a scissor-sharpening service.

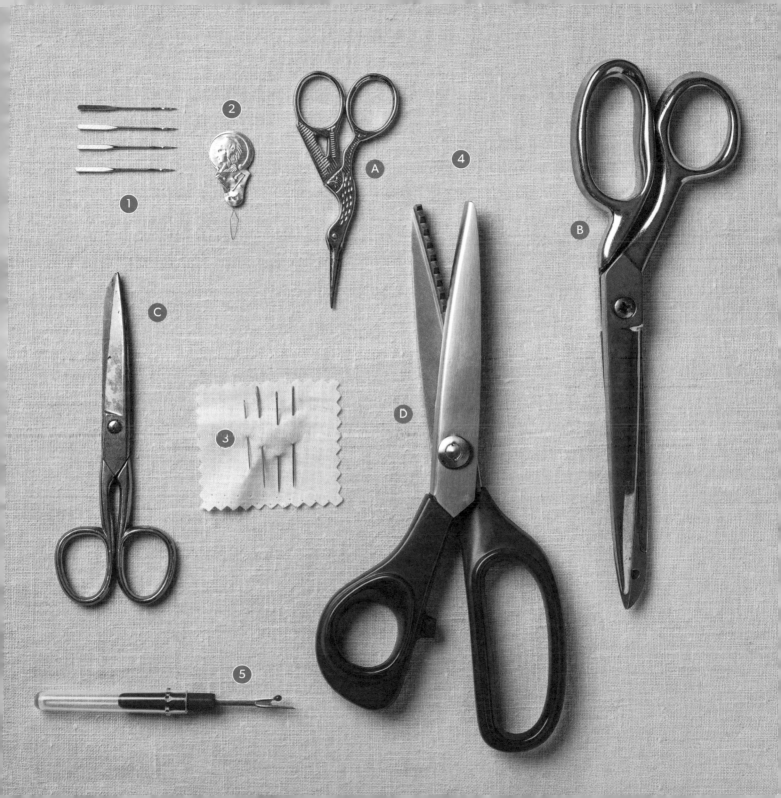

6 PINS

Buy good-quality steel pins that will not rust or become blunt. Keep them in a lidded box. Glass-headed pins are more expensive but very useful as they are easier to see and therefore less likely to become lost in the weave of the fabric.

7 SAFETY PINS

Keep a few safety pins in your sewing kit: they are useful for threading drawstrings through a casing or for holding layers of fabric together, as an alternative to dressmaking pins.

8 PINCUSHION

Keep a pincushion next to the sewing machine, so there is somewhere safe to place pins as you remove them from the fabric. You may want to keep a second pincushion by the ironing board, for the same reason.

9 MARKERS

Tailor's chalk E – a flat square or triangular shaped block – and chalk pencils F, with a brush on the end for erasing chalk marks – are the traditional marking tools for sewing. They are available in various colours; choose a light colour for dark fabrics and vice versa.

An ordinary graphite pencil G is adequate for marking the wrong side of most fabrics. For making marks on the

---

right side of the fabric, which can later be removed, however, look out for an erasable pen H: some types have ink that simply vanishes after a period of time, while others can be erased with water.

10 MEASURING DEVICES

A tape measure I is an essential tool for all sewers, but you will also find a long ruler J useful for drawing lines accurately. Keep a short ruler handy for measuring small areas such as seam allowances. A seam gauge K is a special little ruler, handy for accurately measuring seam allowances, and measuring and marking hems and casings. A set square L is very useful for measuring neat right-angled corners.

---

11 EMBROIDERY HOOP

Essential for holding fabric taut when machine embroidering, hoops come in a variety of sizes. There are several types of hoop available, including one with a spring clip (quick release) and the type shown here, which consists of two wooden rings, the larger of which has a screw that can be tightened or loosened to hold the fabric in place.

IRONING EQUIPMENT

A steam iron is invaluable for pressing your work at various stages. When sewing a project, pressing properly is as important as stitching: it helps to smooth out wrinkles, of course, but it also helps to shape fabric and set seams.

Make sure your ironing-board cover is clean, as dirt and scorch marks can be transferred to your fabric and spoil the appearance.

Always use a pressing cloth when pressing delicate fabrics, and use a scrap of fabric or a piece of kitchen paper to protect the baseplate of your iron from spots of adhesive when using fusible bonding web or fusible interfacing.

BASIC MATERIALS

FABRICS

Fabrics can be made from natural fibres such as cotton, linen, silk or wool, or from plant-based cellulose or synthetic (chemical) fibres.

The projects in this book mostly use medium-weight woven cotton or linen. Woven fabrics are made on a loom. The lengthwise threads are the warp threads and the crosswise threads are the weft. This type of fabric tends to be firm and very stable, and easy to handle and to sew, which is useful if you are a beginner.

Look for craft fabrics – which are often sold for making patchwork and may be bought in small amounts – as well as linen and cotton dress fabrics, and medium-weight washable furnishing fabrics in cotton or a cotton-linen blend.

Natural cotton and linen fabrics have a nicer feel than synthetics and they are available in a multitude of plain colours, stripes, checks and prints. Before cutting and stitching these fabrics, check whether they are pre-shrunk and, if you're not sure, it is advisable to wash and iron them before you do any cutting to allow for shrinking. Make sure you use washable fabrics for items that will be in regular use, such as napkins or a pot holder.

1 PLAIN COTTON

Cotton is the most widely used natural fibre: woven cotton fabric is soft and breathable and very easy to stitch, as the needle passes through the fabric easily.

2 PRINTED COTTON

From spots and stripes to florals, zigzags geometrics, abstracts and novelty motifs, printed fabrics are popular and versatile.

3 TICKING

This heavy, closely woven cotton-twill fabric, used to cover mattresses and cushion pads, usually has a distinctive stripe. It is firm and strong, and a good choice for the oven glove on page 58.

4 GINGHAM

This is a woven cotton dressweight fabric with a regular checked pattern that is often used for school uniforms. These days you are more likely to find gingham in poly-cotton blends.

5 LINEN

This strong fabric is woven from the fibres of the flax plant and usually has a distinctive, sometimes coarse weave.

6 WOVEN CHECKS

Evenly spaced stripes along the length and across the width of a fabric produce a characteristic checked pattern that is a popular and practical choice for home accessories, such as napkins and tablecloths.

7 WOVEN STRIPES

Stripes woven into a fabric are more even than printed stripes, since they follow the weft threads.

8 PLASTICS

Shower-curtain fabric made from PVC can easily be stitched on a sewing machine with an all-purpose needle and makes an ideal wipe-clean lining for the make-up purse on page 74. For heavier plastics, you would need to use a special needle designed for leather and vinyl.

9 WADDING OR BATTING

This soft, non-woven padding material made from synthetic fibres such as polyester, or from cotton, is mainly used as an inner layer for upholstery and quilting.

SEWING THREADS

As a general rule, choose a thread with a fibre content that matches your fabric. Try to match the colour of the fabric as closely as possible or, if an exact match is not possible, choose a shade slightly darker. For tacking (basting), choose a contrasting colour thread that shows up well against the fabric, making it easier to remove.

❶ POLYESTER

Marketed as a 'sew-all' or 'multipurpose' thread, polyester is suitable for most types of fabric. It is available in a choice of thicknesses: choose extra-fine for lightweight fabrics, all-purpose for general sewing, and button or topstitch thread, which is thicker and stronger, for attaching buttons and for decorative topstitching.

❷ MERCERIZED COTTON

Strong and firm, cotton thread is the best choice for cotton and linen fabrics.

❸ EMBROIDERY THREAD

Machine embroidery threads tend to be thicker and more lustrous than sewing threads – and slightly more expensive. They are available in plain, variegated, fluorescent, metallic and glittery colours.

FABRIC AND NEEDLE GUIDE

Different fabrics require different thicknesses of machine needle. Here is a guide to recommended needle sizes for a range of fabrics, along with the optimum stitch length to produce the best results for your sewing projects.

Fabric type	Needle size	Stitches per in/ metric stitch length	
Delicates and sheers (net, voile, lawn, muslin)	fine (8–10)	13–20	2–2.5mm
Lightweight (gingham, dress-weight cottons)	medium (11–14)	13–20	2–2.5mm
Medium (poplin, chintz, linen, ticking)	medium (11–14)	10–12	2.5–3mm
Heavy (denim, twill, velvet, corduroy)	medium–coarse (16–20)	4–5	4.5–5mm

OTHER MATERIALS

1 BIAS BINDING

A narrow strip of fabric, cut on the bias. It is used to bind an edge, to neaten seams, and to cover cords for piping.

2 CORD

Like a twisted rope, cord is available in a number of widths and finishes. Plain white **piping cord** A is usually covered with bias strips to make decorative piping but can also be used to thread through a casing on the top of a drawstring bag, for example. Fancy **coloured cords** B are also used for drawstrings but can be stitched over the seams of a cushion to make a decorative edging.

3 RIBBONS AND TAPES

Thin strips of fabric with bound edges available in a range of widths and finishes, these have a number of practical and decorative uses. **Cotton tape** C can be used to make casings or to thread through casings. **Ribbons** D, usually made from more luxurious materials, are mostly used for decoration and for bows and ties.

WORKING WITH FABRIC

BUYING FABRIC

Fabrics are sold in a number of standard widths. The four most common are 36in (90cm), 44 or 45in (115cm) and 60in (150cm). Consider the width of the fabric when deciding how much to buy, as you may need to buy a longer length to complete a project if your fabric is a narrow width. You will also need to make allowances for the selvedges – the edges of fabric that prevent the fabric from unravelling or fraying. These need to be trimmed off before cutting out fabric pieces for a project.

Fabric amounts are given at the beginning of each project in this book, and care has been taken to avoid waste. For example, the pieces needed for the pintucked cushion cover on page 90 can be cut from a 16in (40cm) length of 44 or 45in (112 or 115cm) fabric.

If only small amounts of fabric are required, consider buying pre-cut pieces such as patchwork squares. Some shops and suppliers sell 'fat quarters': this means that instead of buying a quarter-yard (quarter-metre) cut from the whole width of the fabric, you get a half-yard (half-metre) that is then cut in half up the centre, giving you a piece that is more of a square than a long strip.

Tip Keep to the same type of fabric within a project. You'll need the fabrics to behave in the same way, both while sewing and when washing the finished project afterwards.

MEASURING

When embarking on any home-sewing project, measuring is important to ensure a successful outcome. Accurate measuring is vital when buying fabrics and trimmings, to avoid wastage, and critical at every stage in a sewing project, to make sure that seams line up, hems are straight and the finished item fits properly.

Use a tape measure for measuring items to be covered, such as cushion pads, and for measuring lengths of fabric. A tape measure is flexible, and can be used to measure around curves. When it

---

CUTTING

Accurate cutting is one of the keys to sewing success. Here are a few tips.

- Always cut on a smooth, flat surface.

- Make sure your scissors are sharp.

- Use the full length of the scissor blades for long straight cuts and the tips of the blades, with smaller snips, to cut around curves.

- If you are right-handed, place your left hand on the fabric to stop it from moving around too much.

- Don't use pinking shears to cut out fabric pieces. Instead, use dressmaking shears and, if you wish to pink the edges, do it afterwards, one layer at a time.

comes to measuring seam allowances and hems, however, it is better to use a ruler, since this is rigid and will lie flat, making measurements more accurate.

A seam gauge (see page 22) is even better than a ruler when it comes to seams and hems: look for one with a little slider that you can set to a specific measurement. A long ruler, or yardstick, is also very useful, especially when used in conjunction with a set square, for marking out pieces of fabric.

Tip When measuring fabric, stick with either imperial or metric measurements. Don't use a combination of the two as they are often not exact equivalents.

UNDERSTANDING THE ILLUSTRATIONS

Most stitching is done on the wrong side of the fabric so that when the project is completed, all the stitching is hidden on the inside. It is very important that you follow the illustration guides if you want your stitches and seams to end up in the right place. Use the key below to help you follow the illustrations in this book.

Right side of main fabric

Wrong side of main fabric

Right side of contrast fabric

Wrong side of contrast fabric

Right side of other materials such as interlining or ribbon

Wrong side of other materials such as interlining or ribbon

TECHNIQUES & PROJECTS

Technique one

BASIC MACHINE STITCHES

WHEN THE FIRST DOMESTIC SEWING MACHINES WERE MADE, STRAIGHT STITCH WAS THE ONLY OPTION BUT THE INVENTION OF THE SWING NEEDLE MACHINE ALLOWED ZIGZAG STITCH WITH OTHER VARIATIONS. NOW EVEN THE MOST BASIC MACHINE HAS A GOOD CHOICE OF STITCHES.

TYPES OF STITCH

① STRAIGHT STITCH

Sometimes known as 'lock' stitch, straight stitch is the most basic of all machine stitches. Use it for sewing seams – joining two or more pieces of fabric together – and for hems, darts, topstitching, gathering, machine basting, attaching zippers, binding and piping.

② – ⑥ ZIGZAG STITCH

The machine needle swings from side to side to create an even zigzag stitch. Adjust the stitch width for a narrower or wider zigzag and the stitch length to determine how close together the stitches will be. Zigzag stitch is used for neatening edges, to make buttonholes, and for decorative effects such as appliqué on page 78.

⑦ – ⑧ BLIND-HEM STITCH

Combining a line of straight stitches with zigzags, your machine may offer a number of variations of this stitch, which can be used to sew an 'invisible' hem (you may need to use a blind-hem stitch foot for this), and can also be used to neaten raw edges of fabric.

⑨ CRESCENT OR SCALLOP STITCH

Try altering the stitch length for use as an embroidery or appliqué stitch and for creating decorative edges.

⑩ DECORATIVE STITCHES

Different machines offer different decorative stitches – such as feather stitch – so check your manual to see which stitches are available to you. Some stitches that are intended for sewing stretch fabrics can double up as decorative stitches when worked on plain fabrics.

STITCH LENGTH

Measured in stitches to the inch, or in mm, stitch length needs to be adjusted according to the thickness or weight of your fabric, and whether you are sewing a seam or stitching a gathering thread, for example. If stitches are too short, they tend to pucker the fabric; if they are too long, they will not hold.

STITCH LENGTH GUIDE

These sizes are approximate, so do refer to your machine guide.

Fine fabrics
13–20 stitches per inch   2–2.5mm
Medium fabrics
10–12 stitches per inch   2.5–3mm
Heavy fabrics
4–5 stitches per inch   4.5–5mm
Basting, gathering & topstitching
5–6 stitches per inch   4.5mm

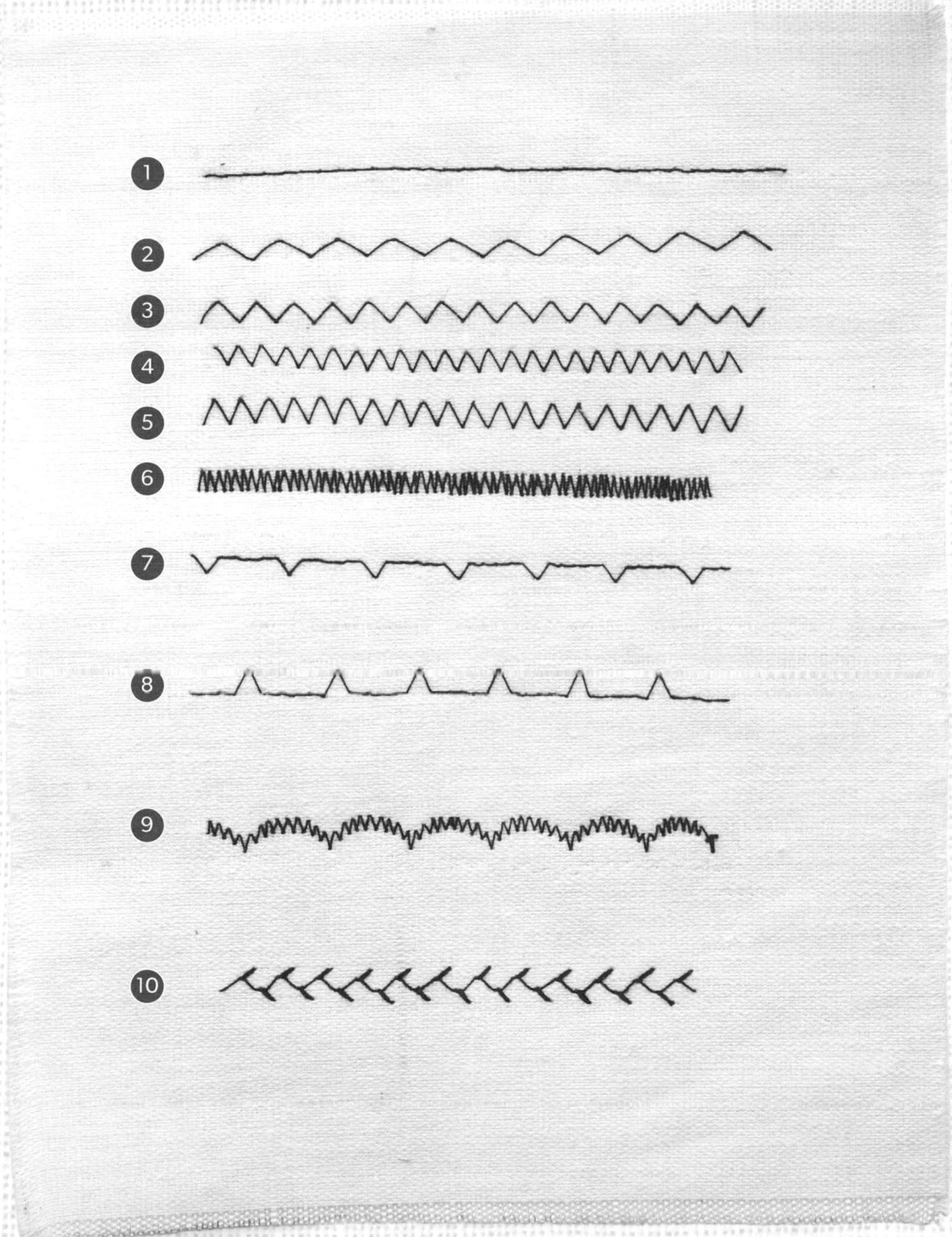
1
2
3
4
5
6
7
8
9
10

Project one

POT HOLDER

GET TO KNOW YOUR SEWING MACHINE BY TRYING OUT THE VARIOUS STITCHES AVAILABLE, THEN TURN YOUR STITCH SAMPLER INTO A USEFUL POT HOLDER. CUSTOMIZE YOUR PROJECT BY CHOOSING YOUR OWN FABRIC AND MATCHING OR CONTRASTING THREAD COLOURS.

YOU WILL NEED

- Medium-weight woven striped fabric, 12in (30cm) square
- Contrast fabric for backing, 12in (30cm) square
- Lightweight polyester wadding, 12in (30cm) square
- White sewing thread
- Ribbon or tape
- Sewing thread in contrast colour, for basting
- Hand-sewing needle
- Scissors

FINISHED SIZE

Approximately 10¾in (26cm) square

TECHNIQUE USED

Basic machine stitches (see page 32)

MATERIALS TO USE

Choose a woven striped fabric so that you have straight lines to follow.

Tip Woven striped and checked fabrics are a good choice when you are a machine sewing novice, as they provide you with straight lines to follow as you stitch.

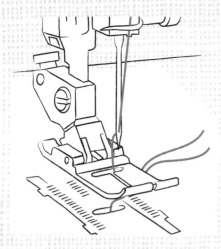 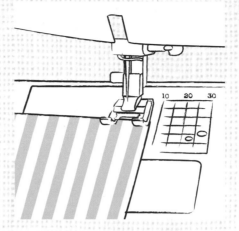 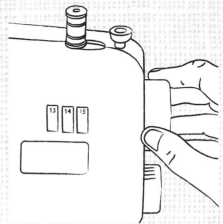

1 Thread the bobbin and the machine with white thread. The ends of both threads should be about 2¼in (6cm). Pass both threads through the slot in the foot and take the ends to one side. Lift the presser foot and turn the hand wheel to raise the needle to its highest point. Switch on the machine.

2 Place the striped fabric square on the machine, under the needle and under the foot, with the raw edges aligned with the ⅝in (15mm) seam line on the throat plate and the top edge of the fabric approximately ⅝in (15mm) behind the needle.

3 Lower the presser foot and make sure the needle is clear of the fabric before selecting your first stitch. Adjust the stitch length to 10 sts per in (2.5mm) and the stitch width to 0. Use the hand wheel to lower the needle into the fabric.

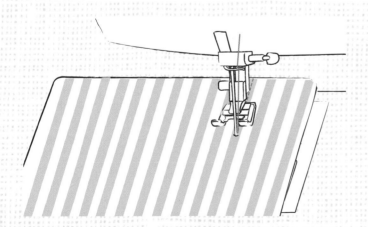

4 Sew down the length of one of the stripes. Follow the line on the throat plate to sew a straight line. Go slowly and steadily, and vary the speed of the machine by adjusting the pressure on the foot control. As you complete a line of stitching, ease off the foot control. Stop before you reach the end of the fabric and complete the last stitches by turning the hand wheel.

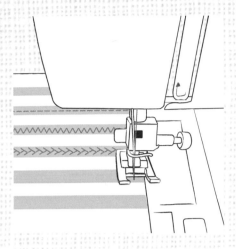
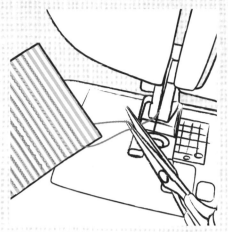
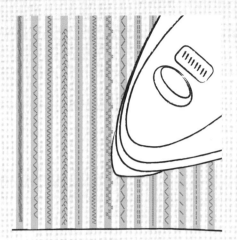

5 Leave the needle in the fabric, lift the presser foot and turn the work by 90°, then lower the presser foot and stitch along the edge until you reach the next stripe. Turn the hand wheel to raise the needle before selecting a new stitch or stitch length. Change the stitch to zigzag and sew down the length of the next stripe. Continue in this way, changing not only the style of stitch but also its length and width.

6 When each of the coloured stripes has a row of stitches along its length, remove the fabric from the machine. To do this, turn the hand wheel to raise the needle to its highest point, lift the presser foot and draw the fabric back until there is about 3in (75mm) of thread. Cut the threads quite close to the fabric.

7 You do not need to secure the thread at the end of the last line of stitching to stop it unravelling because the ends will be enclosed within the seam allowance (see page 48). Press the work on the reverse side of the fabric.

Tip Each time you change the stitch, it is important to lift the needle out of the fabric. To do this, turn the hand wheel to raise the needle.

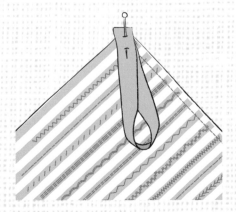

8 Place the stitched fabric right side up on the work surface. Cut a length of tape or ribbon measuring approximately 8in (20cm), place one end on top of the other and pin to one corner of the fabric.

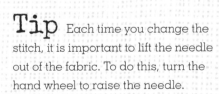

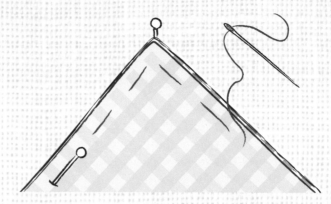

9   Place the backing fabric right side down on top of the stitched fabric, then the wadding on top of the backing fabric. Line up all edges, then pin the layers together.

10   Using a hand-sewing needle with contrasting thread, and large stitches, sew all the layers together about ½in (12mm) from the fabric edges; this is known as basting.

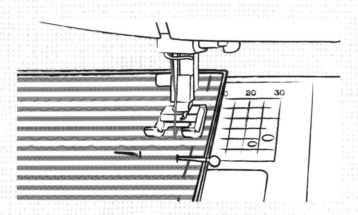

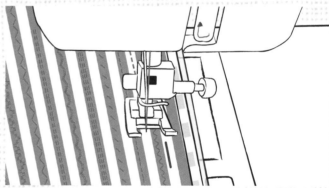

11   Remove the pins and put the work back on the machine, under the needle and under the foot. Make sure the wadding layer is underneath as the surface is not smooth and the fibres will get caught up and snagged in the presser foot when you are machining. Select the reverse stitching option on your machine or leave the needle down and change the direction of the fabric. Then, starting 3in (8cm) from one corner, reverse stitch a few stitches to secure (fasten off) the end of the stitching.

12   Change the setting on your machine to sew forward. Machine ⅝in (15mm) from the raw edges around all sides. Do not stitch on top of the basting but beside it so that it can be removed easily afterwards. Stop stitching 3in (8cm) after the last corner and fasten off. This will leave a gap of about 5½in (14cm) on one side. Remove the fabric from the machine and cut the threads.

REDUCING BULK

If there are several layers of fabric, you can reduce the bulk in the seam by trimming any non-fraying fabrics close to the stitch line, or by trimming away some of the seam allowance on fraying fabrics using pinking shears (as shown below). Snip off corners with a diagonal cut.

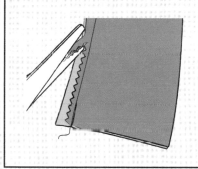

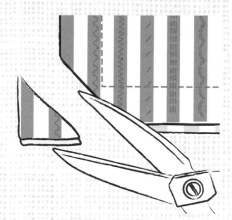

13 Remove the basting by holding one end of the coloured thread and gently pulling it out of the material. Snip across each corner diagonally to reduce excess bulk, and press, then turn right sides out.

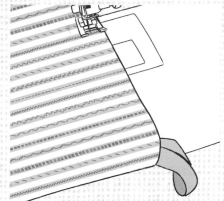

14 Turn under the seam allowance on the opening by ⅝in (15mm). Topstitch (see below) all round the pot holder, about ¼in (6mm) from the edge. Fasten off by reverse stitching a few stitches when you reach the end. Remove the fabric from the machine and cut the threads.

Tip Before you start work on any project, stitch a sample on a spare piece of the fabric you will be working with, to check that the stitch length, width and tension are all suitable.

TOPSTITCHING

Topstitching adds a decorative detail and emphasizes seams and edgings for a really crisp finish. It helps to hold seam allowances flat and can create a neat edging – for example, when worked around the edge of a pocket. Topstitching is worked on the right side of the fabric, usually with a longer stitch than would be used for a seam. You can use the same weight and colour of thread that you used for stitching the seams, or you can use a heavier thread in the same colour or a contrasting one. Before topstitching your project, try out the stitching on a piece of spare fabric folded in half so that there are two layers.

HEMS AND MITRED CORNERS

A HEM IS THE MOST COMMON WAY OF FINISHING OFF AN EDGE. THE EDGE OF THE FABRIC IS FOLDED TO THE WRONG SIDE AND STITCHED IN PLACE. A MITRED CORNER IS THE NEATEST WAY TO SEW THE HEM ON AN ITEM THAT HAS SQUARE CORNERS, SUCH AS A PLACE MAT.

The simplest hem is a single hem, folded to the wrong side and stitched in place. This leaves a raw edge on the wrong side of the fabric which is fine if it is to be covered up with a lining but looks untidy on, say, the lower edge of an unlined curtain or a skirt. By folding a second time, to make a double hem, the raw edge will be enclosed. For the neatest results, press before and after stitching.

For most sewing projects, and for most garments, a hem that is between ½in and 1½in (12mm and 38mm) is about right: wide enough to neaten the edge without fraying. For curtains, however, hems sometimes need to be much wider than this, so that they add a bit of weight and help the fabric to hang well. And for items made from very fine, fragile fabrics, hems usually need to be very narrow.

Tip A narrow hem is ideal for lightweight garments, sheer curtains and table linen; a deeper hem gives weight to the bottom of a curtain.

HOW TO SEW A DOUBLE HEM

To make a double hem, you fold over
the edge twice and secure it with
stitching. Make the hem narrow or deep,
depending on what you are making.

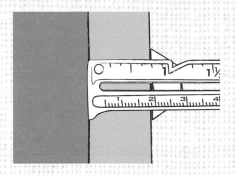

1 Fold the raw edge over to the
wrong side. For a narrow hem, you
could turn over ⅜–¾in (1–2cm) – use
a seam gauge (or ruler) to ensure
that the hem is even. Press the
folded edge.

2 Fold again, the same amount or
slightly more; press.

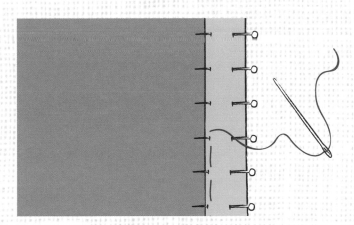

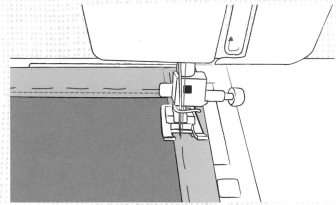

3 Pin, to hold the folds in place, and then baste, using a hand-
sewing needle with contrasting thread, and large stitches.

4 Remove the pins. Secure the end and machine stitch
the hem in place, close to the inside fold. Fasten off, and
remove the fabric from the machine. Remove the basting
stitches and press again.

MITRING A CORNER

For the neatest finish where a hem goes round a corner, learn to do a mitre. This is easy as long as you follow the process carefully, and looks very professional.

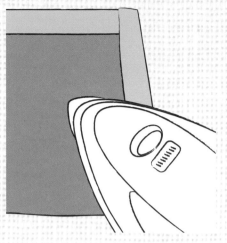

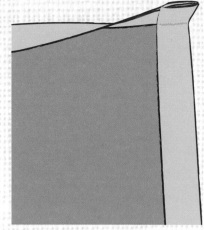

1 Fold a single hem on all four sides of the fabric, and press.

2 Fold over again to make a double hem, and press.

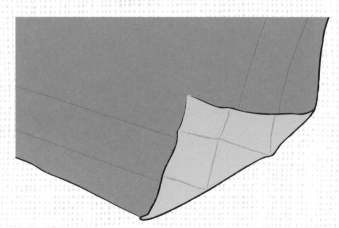

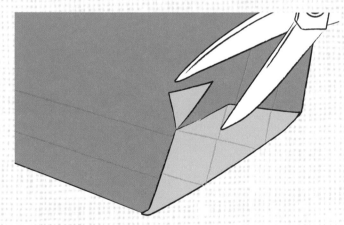

3 Open out the folds. On one corner, turn back the corner to form a neat right-angled triangle, with the folds lining up.

4 Turn back the point of the corner to meet the centre of the diagonal fold and press. Trim off this corner along the fold you have just made.

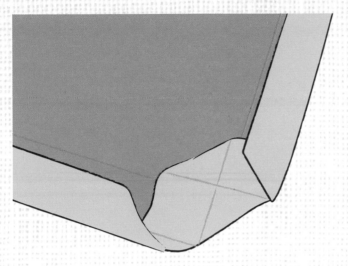

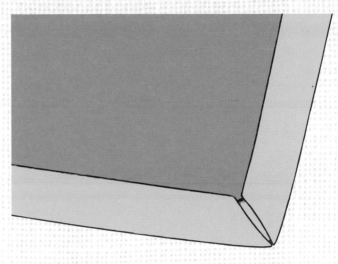

5 Fold the first part of the hem again, along the original fold lines.

6 Fold the second part of the hem; the corner edges should meet in a neat diagonal. Pin and baste to hold in place.

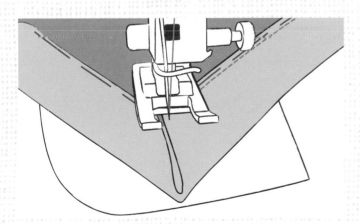

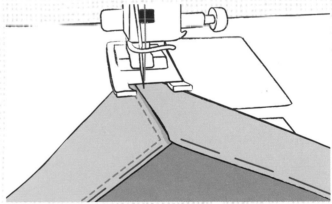

7 Remove the pins. Stitch along the hem, close to the inner fold, until you reach the corner, then stitch down the first edge of the mitre.

8 When you reach the outer corner, lower the needle into the fabric, lift the presser foot and swivel the fabric, then lower the presser foot and stitch along the other edge of the mitre, then continue stitching the hem. Fasten off and remove the fabric from the machine. Remove the basting.

PLACE SETTINGS

PRACTISE NEAT HEMMING ON PIECES OF WOVEN CHECK FABRIC TO CREATE A MATCHING SET OF NAPKINS, PLACE MATS AND A TRAY CLOTH. THIS IS ALSO AN OPPORTUNITY TO BECOME EXPERIENCED IN CREATING THE PERFECT NEATLY MITRED CORNER.

YOU WILL NEED

- Woven check fabric (see 'Materials to use' for quantities)
- Printed cotton fabric, for backing place mats
- Sewing thread to match fabrics
- Sewing thread in contrast colour, for basting
- Hand-sewing needle

FINISHED SIZE

Napkin: 8¾ x 8¾in (22 x 22cm)
Place mat: 12¼ x 8¼in (31 x 21cm)
Tray cloth: 16 x 8¼in (40.5 x 21cm)

TECHNIQUES USED

Straight stitch (see page 32)
Hems (see page 40)
Mitring a corner (see page 40)

MATERIALS TO USE

A woven check cotton fabric is a good choice for this project because the lines of the pattern act as an accurate guide for cutting and folding.

A 20-in (half-metre) length of woven check fabric, 60in (150cm) wide, is enough to make four napkins, four place mats and a tray cloth.

1 Cut off the selvedges on either side of your fabric and discard them.

2 Measure and cut out a 10in (25cm) square for each napkin. Make them a little larger or smaller than this if it means cutting along the edge of a line of squares. Cut a rectangle of fabric 14 x 10in (35 x 25cm) for each place mat. Cut a rectangle approximately 18 x 13in (45 x 34cm) for a tray cloth, adjusting these measurements if necessary to fit a particular tray.

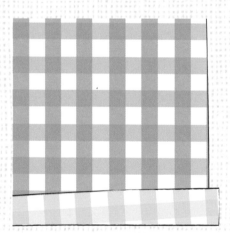

3 Take a piece of fabric and fold over a single hem ⅝in (15mm) wide (or as wide as one or two rows of squares, if you find this easier.

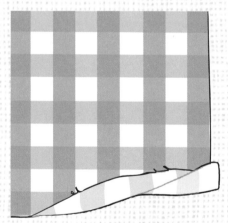

4 Open out the hem and fold the raw edge to the foldline, to create a double hem.

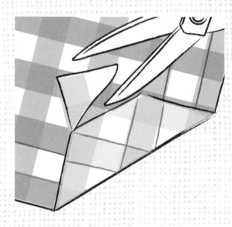

5 Open out the hem. On one corner, fold the corner to form a neat right-angled triangle, with the folds lining up. Fold back the point of the corner to meet the centre of the diagonal fold and press. Trim off this corner along the fold you have just made. Repeat on the other corners.

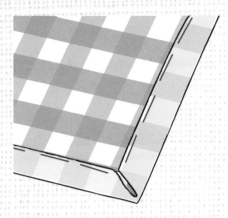

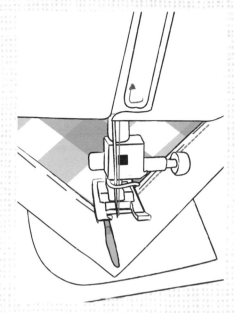

7 Stitch along the hem, close to the inner fold, to the corner, then stitch down the first edge of the mitre. When you reach the outer corner, lower the needle into the fabric, lift the presser foot, swivel the fabric, then lower the presser foot and stitch along the other edge of the mitre, then continue stitching the hem until you reach the starting point. Fasten off, remove from the machine, and remove the basting. Repeat steps 3–7 for all pieces of fabric; at this point you will have completed the napkins and tray cloth.

6 Fold the first part of the hem again, along the original fold lines. Fold the second part of the hem; the corner edges should meet in a neat diagonal. Pin, then baste in place.

HAND-SEWN CORNERS

To make mitred corners extra neat, you may prefer to sew them by hand, slipstitching the diagonal folded edges together.

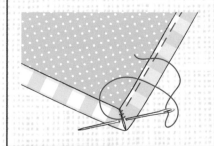

8 To make a place mat, cut a piece of backing fabric measuring 13 x 9½in (34 x 24cm). Place the backing fabric centrally on the main place-mat fabric, wrong sides together.

9 Fold over the hem and mitre the corners, as described in steps 3–7, and press, then machine stitch the hem all round. Fasten off. Repeat steps 8 and 9 to make all the place mats.

SEAMS

LEARN HOW TO SEW A STRAIGHT SEAM AND YOU CAN CREATE A WHOLE RANGE OF ITEMS, INCLUDING CUSHIONS, BAGS AND GARMENTS. THE SEAM IS THE BASIS OF ALL MACHINE SEWING PROJECTS AND TIME INVESTED IN MASTERING THE TECHNIQUE WILL PAY DIVIDENDS.

A seam, in its simplest form, is simply a line of straight stitching used to join two pieces of fabric. This is where the sewing machine earns its price, as you can machine sew a straight, strong seam far more quickly than you could by hand. There are many types of seam and seam finish, but they all start with the same basic technique shown here.

SEAM ALLOWANCES

A standard seam allowance is ⅝ in (15mm). You should find a marking for this on the throat plate of your sewing machine; align the edges of your fabric to the marking. If your machine does not have this marking, you can place a piece of masking tape this distance from the needle, to use as a sewing guide.

Tip Before you start work on any project, always stitch a sample using two scraps of the fabric and the thread you will be working with. Adjust the tension and stitch length, as necessary, for a perfect seam.

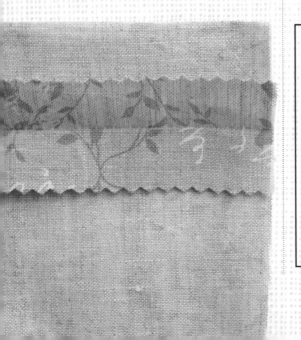

SIMPLE SEAM FINISHES

To prevent the raw edges of fabrics fraying, trim them with pinking shears, as shown here, or machine stitch along the raw edge using a zigzag stitch (see page 32).

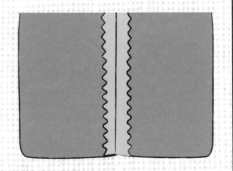

HOW TO SEW A SIMPLE SEAM

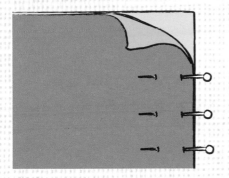

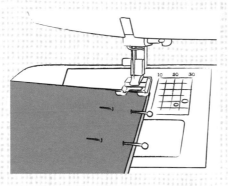

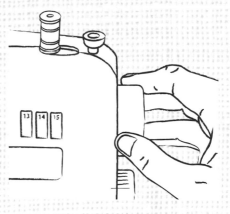

1 Place two pieces of fabric, right sides together, with the raw edges aligned. Pin the fabric edges together, inserting the pins at right angles to the edge.

2 Place the fabric on the machine, under the needle and under the foot, with the raw edges aligned with the ⅝in (15mm) seam line on the throat plate and the top edge of the fabric approximately ⅝in (15mm) behind the needle.

3 Lower the presser foot and set the machine to straight stitch. Adjust the stitch length to 10 sts per in (2.5mm). Use the hand wheel to lower the needle into the fabric.

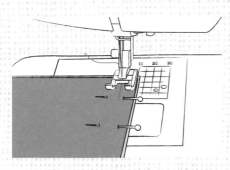

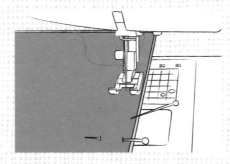

4 Select the reverse stitching option on your machine or leave the needle down and change the direction of the fabric. Starting about ½in (12mm) from the edge, sew in reverse and stitch to the top edge of the fabric to secure the start of the seam.

5 Now sew forwards and stitch down the length of the seam, removing the pins as you go; backstitch a few stitches to fasten off at the end. Remove the fabric from the machine (see page 37).

6 Press the seam open, on the wrong side; turn the fabric over and press again, on the right side of the fabric.

Project three

STRIP QUILT

JOIN STRIPS OF FABRIC TOGETHER TO MAKE A SPEEDY PATCHWORK QUILT IN A FRACTION OF THE TIME IT WOULD TAKE TO SEW BY HAND. THESE INSTRUCTIONS ARE FOR A SMALL QUILT BUT YOU CAN ENLARGE EACH STRIP, OR ADD EXTRA STRIPS OF FABRIC, TO CREATE A LARGER QUILT.

YOU WILL NEED

- Cotton fabrics in five different prints, each 30 x 10in (75 x 25cm)
- Printed cotton fabric, 51 x 33½in (130 x 85cm), for backing
- Lightweight polyester wadding, 47 x 10in (120 x 75cm)
- Sewing thread to match fabrics
- Sewing thread in contrast colour, for basting
- Hand-sewing needle

FINISHED SIZE

The finished quilt measures 47 x 30in (120 x 75cm), making it an ideal shape and size for a lap quilt or a coverlet for a baby's cot, and small enough to be portable – to take on a picnic or a trip to the beach.

TECHNIQUES USED

Basic machine stitches (see page 32)
Hems (see page 40)
Seams (see page 48)

MATERIALS TO USE

Fabric amounts given here are the exact size needed for the rectangular strips that make up the quilt top. The measurements for the wadding and the backing fabric are slightly larger, to allow for trimming at the appropriate stage.

Craft cotton is a good choice for a patchwork project like this. It is usually available in a 44in (110cm) width, so if you are buying fabric from the roll and the retailer sells the fabric in short lengths, you may be able to buy exactly 10in (25cm) of each of the prints used for the quilt top. If you have to buy more, you can save any leftover scraps for future projects.

Make sure that the fabric you buy is washable, so that the finished quilt can be laundered. Also check whether it is pre-shrunk; if not, it is advisable to wash and iron all the fabrics before sewing them together.

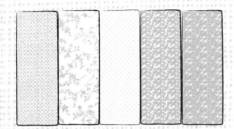

1 Arrange the five pieces of fabric you are using for the quilt top, with long edges aligned, on a large flat surface.

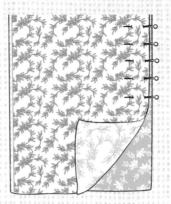

2 Take the first two pieces and place right sides together, aligning the edges to be joined. Pin these pieces together, inserting the pins at right angles to the edge.

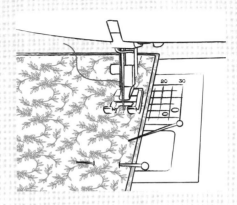

3 Backstitch to the top edge of the fabric to secure the end. Stitch the two pieces together, with a ⅜in (1cm) seam, removing each pin as you come to it.

4 Join the other pieces in the same way, to complete the top of the quilt. Press the seams open. Do this from the wrong side, then turn the fabric over and press the seams again on the right side.

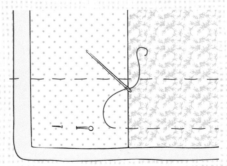

5 Place the wadding on the work surface and place the quilt top centrally on top of the wadding. Pin the two layers of fabric together, then baste, using a hand-sewing needle with contrasting thread, and large stitches.

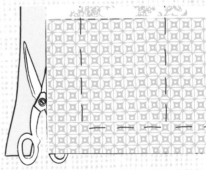

6 Trim away excess wadding, close to the fabric edge. Place the backing fabric wrong side up on the work surface, then the basted wadding and quilt top centrally on top. Baste through all three layers, about ½in (12mm) from the raw edges.

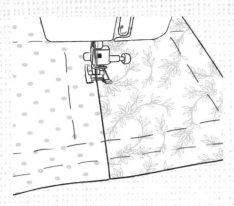

7 Topstitch (see page 39) along the join between each fabric strip. Remove the work from the machine. Take out the basting stitches and press the work.

8 Measure and cut the backing, with a margin of 2in (5cm) all round. Fold the corner of the backing fabric to the corner of the main fabric, then cut along the fold line.

9 Fold the cut edge of the backing fabric twice, letting it overlap the corner of the cover.

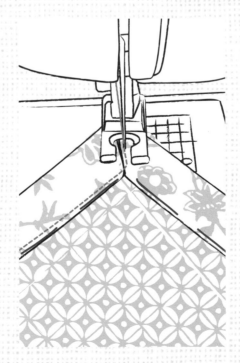

10 Fold the edge of the backing to meet the edge of the quilt top and batting, then fold the folded edge in to the same point. Now fold this over the edge of the top fabric. Pin it in position, then baste.

11 Topstitch close to the inner edge of the border. When you come to a corner, leave the needle in the fabric, lift the presser foot and turn the work; lower the presser foot and stitch down the edge of the diagonal fold to the corner; swivel the fabric again and stitch back to the first turning point. Swivel the work again, and continue stitching to the next corner. Repeat for all corners. Fasten off the end, remove from the work from the machine and press.

BINDING AND PIPING

BIAS STRIPS CAN BE USED IN A VARIETY OF PRACTICAL WAYS: TO FINISH EDGES, TO NEATEN SEAMS AND TO JOIN PIECES DECORATIVELY. BUY READY-MADE BINDING OR CUT YOUR OWN FABRIC STRIPS TO MATCH OR CO-ORDINATE WITH YOUR MAIN FABRIC.

BIAS BINDING

Bound edges are a useful alternative to hemming, especially when layers of different fabrics are involved, such as when making a quilt. Binding gives a neat finish and can create less bulk than a hem.

The technique involves using bias strips of fabric that have been folded. As fabric cut on the bias is slightly stretchy, it can be eased around shaped edges.

Bias binding can be purchased in several standard widths, in cotton, poly-cotton or satin finishes, and in a range of colours and prints. If you wish to match a particular colour or print, however, you can make your own by cutting strips of fabric on the bias then folding in the edges, which is easier to do if you have a little gadget known as a bias tape maker (see below).

BIAS TAPE MAKER

This useful gadget helps to fold both edges of a bias strip neatly and evenly. To use it, cut the end of the bias strip diagonally, then feed it into the device. As the folded strip emerges from the tip, press it with a hot iron. The device has a loop on top, which you pull with one hand, gently and slowly, as you hold the iron with the other hand. Make sure you purchase the bias tape maker that is the right one for the tape size you want to make.

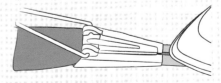

BINDING AN EDGE

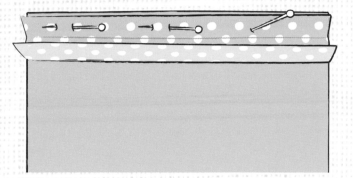

1 Open out one of the folded edges of the bias binding and place it along the edge of the fabric, with the right sides together and raw edges matching. Pin in place.

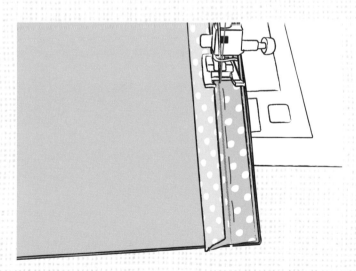

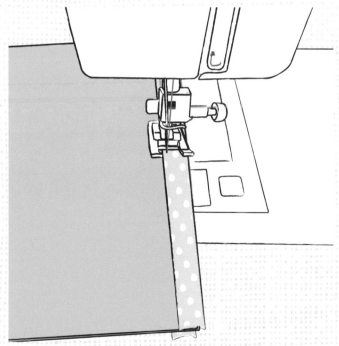

2 Baste the binding in place, just above the fold line, and remove the pins. Stitch along the fold line, using thread that matches the binding.

3 Fold the binding over the fabric edge to the wrong side, and line up the folded edge of the binding with the stitch line. Topstitch, close to the folded edge.

Piping cord is available to buy in a range of standard widths, with measurements referring to the diameter of the cord.

The most commonly available widths of bias binding are ½in (12mm) and 1in (25mm). The narrower width is ideal for finishing raw edges on light or medium-weight fabrics; use the wider width for multiple layers of fabric, especially if there is a layer of wadding.

COVERED PIPING CORD

Piped seams can be used as a decorative device when joining two pieces of fabric, helping to accentuate the joins. Buy covered piping cord or make your own.

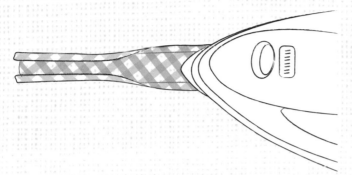

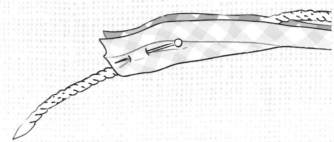

1 Cut a strip of fabric on the bias or, if you are using commercial bias binding, press it open.

2 Place a length of piping cord on the wrong side of the binding and bring up the edges of the binding to cover the cord. With the edges of the binding aligned, pin through both thicknesses, close to the cord.

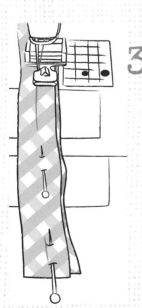

3 Fit the sewing machine with a zipper foot; this allows you to stitch close to the cord for a neat result. Stitch the piping in place, using a straight stitch, removing each pin as you come to it.

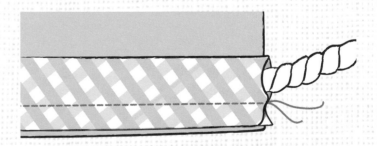

4 To add piping to a seam, line up the edges of the binding to the edge of the fabric, pin and baste, then machine close to the cord. Add the second piece of fabric on top, lining up fabric edges as before, and stitch again. Remove basting.

OVEN GLOVE

PROTECT YOUR HANDS FROM HOT POTS AND PANS – AND PRACTISE PIPING AND BINDING TECHNIQUES AT THE SAME TIME – WITH THIS SIMPLE, PRACTICAL OVEN GLOVE. USE WASHABLE FABRICS THAT MATCH YOUR KITCHEN COLOUR SCHEME.

YOU WILL NEED

- 12in (30cm) mattress ticking, 57in (145cm) wide
- 8in (20cm) backing fabric, 57in (145cm) wide
- 16in (40cm) of ¼in (6mm) piping cord
- 16in (40cm) white bias binding, ⅝in (15mm) wide
- 8¼ft (2.5m) blue bias binding, 1in (25mm) wide
- Lightweight polyester wadding, 55 x 8in (140 x 20cm)
- Sewing thread to match binding
- Sewing thread in contrast colour, for basting
- Hand-sewing needle

FINISHED SIZE

34 x 7in (86 x 18 cm)

TECHNIQUES USED

Basic machine stitches (see page 32)
Hems (see page 40)
Seams (see page 48)
Binding (see page 54)
Piping (see page 56)

MATERIALS TO USE

Mattress ticking is a good choice for a project like this. It is usually available in a 57in (145cm) width, with the stripes running along the length of the fabric. If you are buying fabric from the roll and the fabric is sold in short lengths, you will need to buy only 12in (30cm), as the project is designed so that pieces are cut and joined to ensure that the stripes run down the length of the oven glove without the need to buy too much fabric.

1 Cut three rectangles, each 7in (18cm) wide, from the mattress ticking, cutting along the stripes.

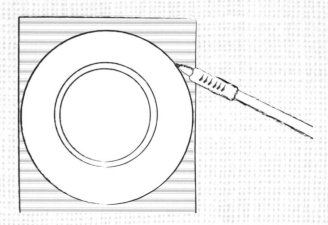

2 Place two of these pieces on top of one another, pin together, then place a round object such as a bowl or small plate, approximately 7in (18cm) in diameter, on top, towards one end, and draw around half of it, to create a curved edge on the fabric.

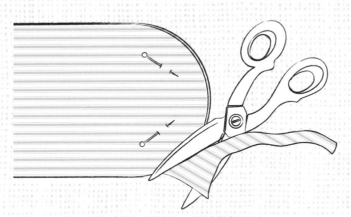

3 Cut through both thicknesses of fabric, along this line. These form the two end pieces for the oven glove.

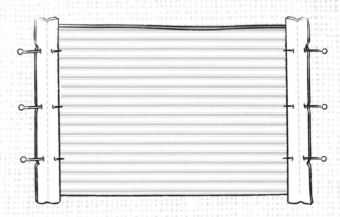

4 Fit a zipper foot to your sewing machine. Cover the piping cord with white bias binding (see page 57). Cut the bound piping into two equal lengths, each approximately 8in (20cm) long, and pin one to each short edge of the middle section of the oven glove, on the right side of the fabric.

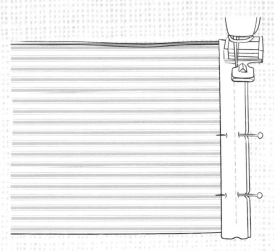

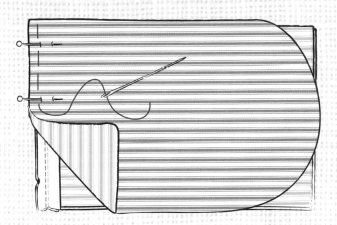

5 Reverse stitch to secure the end then machine stitch the piping in place, close to the cord, removing each pin as you come to it. Fasten off and remove the work from the machine. Trim off the excess piping on either side of the fabric.

6 Place the short edge of each end piece of the oven glove on top of the binding and pin in place. Baste if you wish to. Machine stitch close to the cord and fasten off. Do the same with the other curved end piece. Press.

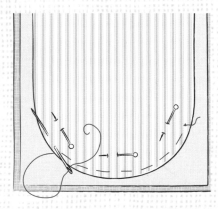

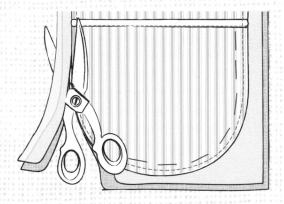

7 Place the backing fabric on the work surface, wrong side up, place the wadding on top, then the joined fabric right side up on top of the wadding. Pin the three layers together, then baste close to the edge.

8 Machine stitch to join all three layers, using the regular foot on the sewing machine and stitching about ¼in (6mm) from the edge of the main fabric. Trim away excess wadding and backing, close to the fabric edge. Remove the basting.

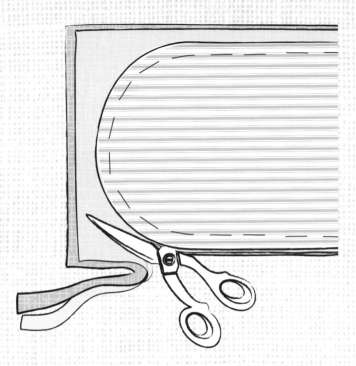

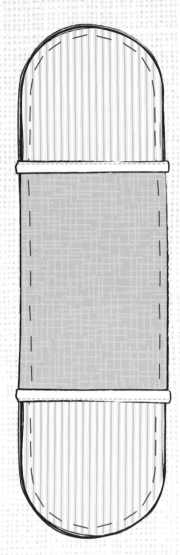

9 To make pockets, cut two pieces of mattress ticking, each measuring 9 x 7in (23 x 18cm), with stripes running along the length of each piece. Cut one short end of each in a curve, as described in step 2. Cut two pieces of backing fabric and two pieces of wadding, slightly larger than the ticking pieces; place the backing on the work surface, wrong side up, followed by the wadding and ticking. Pin and baste through all three layers, then machine stitch and trim away excess, as described in step 8.

10 Bind the straight edge of each of the pocket pieces (see page 55). Place the main piece of the oven glove on the work surface, with the backing side uppermost. Place one pocket at each end, right sides up. Baste around the two curved ends, through all layers.

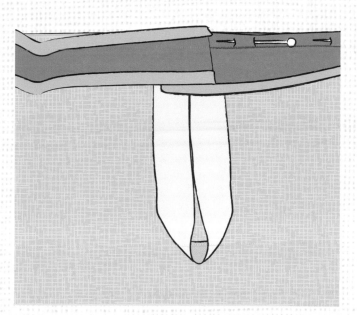

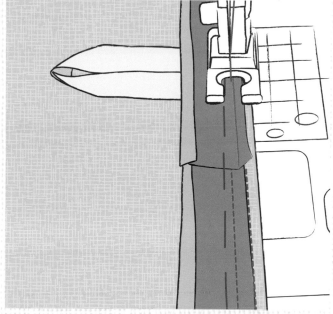

11. Pin the binding all round the perimeter of the oven glove. Fold the plain cotton tape in half and place it in the centre of one long side, with the two ends tucked under the binding.

12. Baste the binding in place, if you wish, then machine stitch along the fold line.

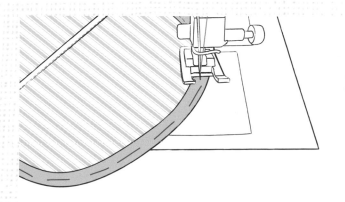

13. Fold the binding over to cover the raw edges, line up the folded edge with the stitchline, then pin and baste. Remove the pins and topstitch all around the work. Fasten off, remove the oven glove from the machine and remove the basting. Press.

CASINGS

A CASING IS A KIND OF 'TUNNEL' OF FABRIC OR TAPE THROUGH WHICH YOU CAN THREAD A CORD, RIBBON OR ELASTIC, TO MAKE DRAWSTRINGS, FOR EXAMPLE. THESE CAN BE USED ON CLOTHING, TO GATHER FULLNESS, OR ON THE TOP OF A BAG TO CLOSE UP THE OPENING.

FOLDED CASING

Create a casing on the top edge of a waistband or bag by folding over the fabric to form a wide double hem, then topstitching to create a channel through which to thread a drawstring.

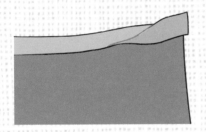

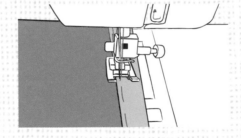

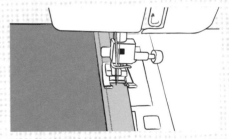

1 Fold over a deep double hem, and press the folded edges. Make sure it is wider than the ribbon, cord or elastic that will be threaded through. Pin and baste in place.

2 Machine stitch the hem in place, close to the fold. Remove the basting stitches and press again.

3 Decide how wide you wish the channel to be, based on the width of your drawstring but with an additional ⅛in (2mm), then topstitch this distance from the previous line of stitching, making sure you secure the ends at the beginning and end of sewing.

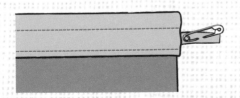

4 Thread your drawstring through the channel. If you secure a safety pin at one end it will be easier to pull through the channel.

SEPARATE CASING

Alternatively, you can make a separate casing by stitching a strip of fabric, with the long edges folded under, or a length of tape or ribbon, on to a piece of fabric.

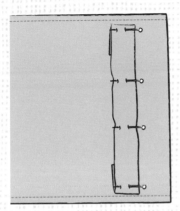

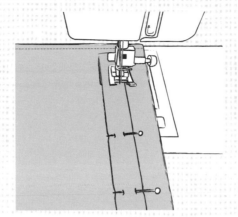

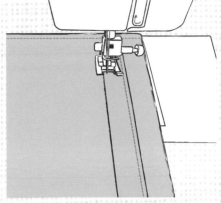

1 Fold under the ends of the tape or strip of fabric and pin in place on the right side of the main fabric. This tape or fabric strip should be as wide as the drawstring, plus about ⅝in (15mm) to allow for stitching.

2 Machine stitch one edge of the casing in place, close to the edge of the tape (about ⅛–¼in/3–6mm), removing the pins as you go. Backstitch at the beginning and end of the stitching to prevent unravelling.

3 Machine stitch the other side of the casing, stitching in the same direction as the first side.

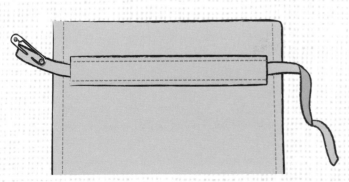

4 Thread ribbon or cord through the channel.

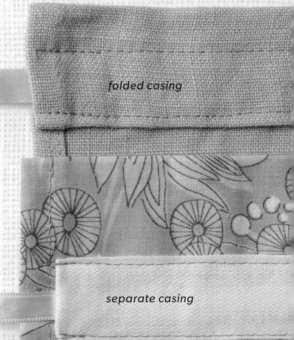

folded casing

separate casing

DRAWSTRING BAG

ONCE YOU HAVE DISCOVERED JUST HOW EASY AND QUICK THESE BAGS ARE TO MAKE, AND HOW USEFUL AND PRACTICAL THEY ARE, YOU'LL BE MAKING LOTS MORE IN ALL SORTS OF SHAPES, SIZES AND FABRICS.

YOU WILL NEED
- Printed cotton fabric, 28 x 11in (70 x 28cm)
- Contrast cotton fabric, 12 x 10½in (30 x 26cm)
- Cotton fabric, 4in (10cm) square, to neaten cord ends
- 55in (1.4m) of ¼in (6mm) cord
- Sewing thread to match fabric
- Sewing thread in contrast colour, for basting
- Hand-sewing needle

FINISHED SIZE
15½ x 10in (39 x 25cm)

TECHNIQUES USED
Hems (see page 40)
Seams (see page 48)
Casings (see page 64)

Tip Because this bag is unlined, you may wish to neaten the seams to prevent fraying. There are tips showing various ways to do this on page 48.

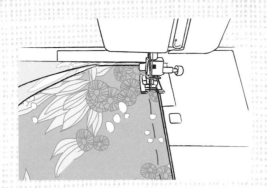

1 Fold the main fabric in half, right sides together. Stitch both side seams, with a ⅝in (15mm) seam allowance, to within ⅜in (10mm) of the top edge. Turn the right sides out and press.

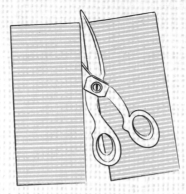

2 Cut the contrast fabric in half so that you have two pieces, each measuring 11¾ x 5⅛in (30 x 13cm), for the top casing.

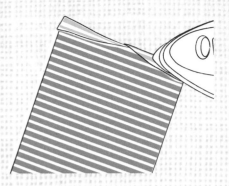

3 Stitch a double hem on the short ends of the two casing pieces. To do this, fold ⅜in (10mm) to wrong side and press, then fold another ⅝in (15mm) to the wrong side and press again. Measure accurately as this will ensure that each casing is the same length as the width of the bag, for a neat result.

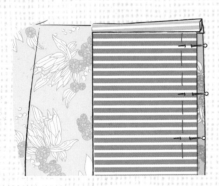

4 On the right side of the bag front, line up one long edge of one of the casing pieces, wrong side uppermost, with the top (unfinished) edge of the bag, pin and baste. Do the same with the other piece.

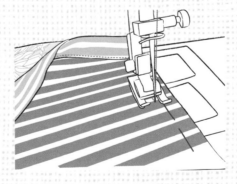

5 Remove the pins. Secure the end of the stitching and stitch the bag and casings together ⅝in (15mm) from the raw edges. Fasten off and remove the basting. Press the seam to one side, towards the casing.

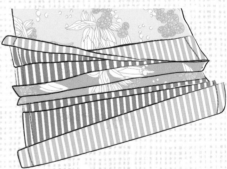

6 Fold under ⅝in (15mm) on the other long edge of the casing and pin to the inside of bag, lining up the fold with the stitch line. Press.

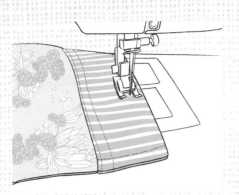

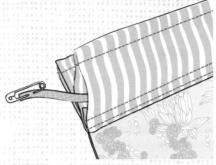

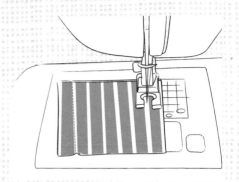

7 Topstitch ⅛in (2mm) from the top fold of the casing. Topstitch again, approximately ³⁄₁₆in (5mm) above the first line of stitching. Topstitch ⅝in (15mm) from the top edge of the casing. Backstitch at the beginning and end of the stitching to prevent the thread unravelling.

8 Cut two 27½in (70cm) lengths of cord and insert into the casing. If you attach a safety pin to the end of the cord it will be easier to pull through. Start each one at opposite ends so that you have two cord ends emerging at each side.

9 Cut a small square of fabric, about 6in (15.25cm), in half to make two 'pockets' or tabs to neaten the ends of the cords. Fold each piece in half, with right sides together, and stitch the side seams with a ³⁄₈in (10mm) seam allowance.

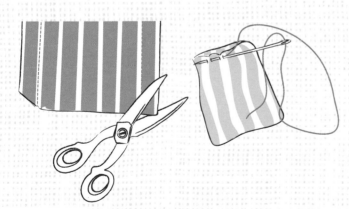

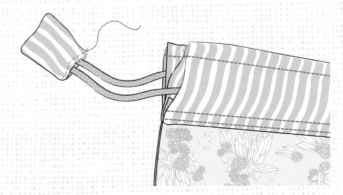

10 Clip the corners and turn the pockets right sides out. Fold the raw edge to the inside, then stitch a running stitch, by hand, around the top, close to the fold.

11 Push the two ends of one of the cords into this little pocket, pull up the threads to gather, and fasten off securely. Do the same with the other pair of cord ends.

ZIPPERS

A ZIPPER IS A PRACTICAL FASTENING FOR ALL KINDS OF PROJECTS, NOT ONLY FOR CLOTHING BUT FOR CUSHIONS AND BAGS. ZIPPERS CAN BE HIDDEN OR CAN BE MADE INTO A FEATURE, DEPENDING ON THE EFFECT YOU WISH TO ACHIEVE.

'Nylon' zippers – which are actually made from polyester – are an inexpensive method of fastening clothing, cushions and bags.

A zipper typically consists of two tapes – each with a row of teeth or coils – with a slider that locks the teeth or coils together and opens them up again.

A robust zipper with nylon or metal teeth is a good choice for soft furnishings, especially where the zipper, or at least part of it, will be exposed.

Polyester zippers are the most common choice. Previously made from nylon, these are still often referred to as 'nylon' zippers.

Open-ended zippers are used for jackets and cardigans, and also for items of soft furnishing, such as sleeping bags.

Invisible zippers have nylon coils instead of teeth, that sit behind the tapes. Inserting an invisible zipper requires a special method that is rather challenging for beginners, so it is wise to stick to a simpler technique like the centred zipper outlined below, or the two-step method used on the make-up purse on page 74.

ZIPPER FOOT

This special foot is narrow, and instead of having a central hole through which the needle passes, it has a notch on each side. This allows the presser foot to get as close as possible to the teeth of the zipper.

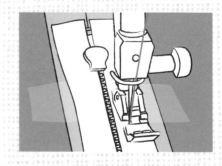

You can choose to make a feature of a zipper or conceal it. The zipper on the left reveals the metal teeth; the nylon coils of the zipper on the right are concealed under narrow flaps of fabric.

INSERTING A CENTRED ZIPPER

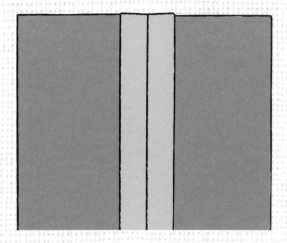

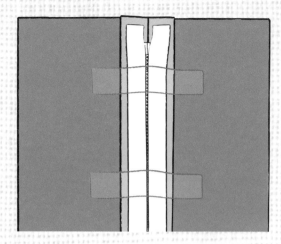

1 The zipper will be positioned in the seam that joins two pieces of fabric. Stitch the seam and press open. The zipper will be positioned on this seam and the stitches in this section unpicked afterwards, to reveal the zipper teeth.

2 Place the zipper face down on the opened seam, with the teeth lying along the stitch line. You can pin and then baste the tapes in place, or you can use short lengths of adhesive tape, which will help to keep the zipper lying flat.

Tip Using sticky tape instead of pins is a quick shortcut but to make sure the zipper fits really well, it is better to invest a little time in hand-basting before machine stitching in place.

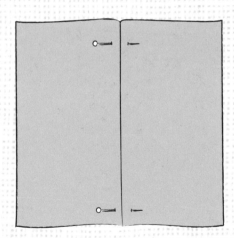

3 On the right side of the fabric, place two pins, to mark the top and bottom of the teeth of the zipper.

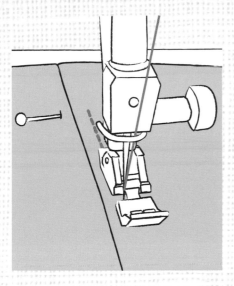

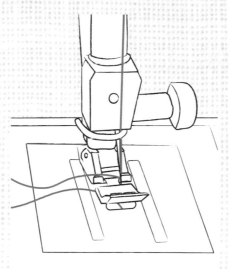

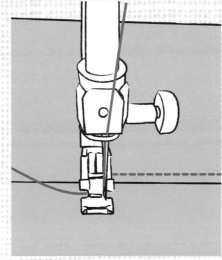

4 Starting at the top pin, on the right side of the zipper, machine stitch down to the position of the second pin. Note that the needle should be aligned with the left-hand notch of the zipper foot.

5 Swap the needle over to the left-hand side of the foot.

6 With the needle in the fabric, lift the presser foot and swivel the fabric so that you can stitch across the bottom edge of the zipper.

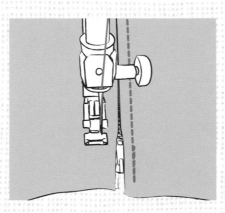

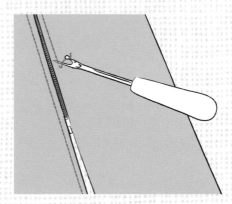

7 After stitching along the bottom, swivel the fabric again and stitch up the other side of the zipper, to the top pin.

8 Use a seam ripper to unpick stitches above the teeth of the zipper.

Project six

MAKE-UP PURSE

IT IS MUCH EASIER THAN YOU MAY THINK TO MAKE A LITTLE PURSE WITH A WIPE-CLEAN
LINING AND ZIPPED CLOSURE IN WHICH TO CARRY COSMETICS. IT'S SO EASY, IN FACT,
THAT YOU CAN MAKE PURSES IN TWO SIZES IN NEXT TO NO TIME AT ALL.

YOU WILL NEED
- Printed cotton fabric, 12 x 8in
  (30.5 x 20cm)
- Transparent PVC fabric, 12 x 8in
  (30.5 x 20cm), for lining
- 7in (18cm) zipper
- Sewing thread to match fabric
- Sewing thread in contrast colour,
  for basting
- Hand-sewing needle
- Set square
- Zipper foot
- Small split ring (optional)
- Metal charm (optional)

FINISHED SIZE
3½in (9cm) long x 2¾in (7cm) wide.
To make a larger version, use a 9in (23cm)
zipper and use 15 x 10in (38 x 25cm) of
fabric and lining.

Tip Attach a small charm to the
zipper pull, using a split ring; this makes
it easier to open and close the zip.

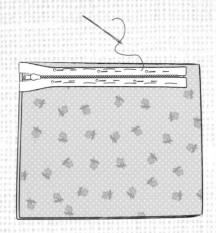

1 Place the PVC lining on the work surface with the main fabric right side up on top. Place the zipper face down at the top, with the tape lined up with the upper edges. Pin in place, then baste by hand using a contrasting thread.

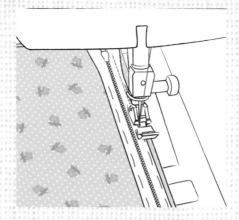

2 Fit the zipper foot to the machine and stitch down the centre of the zipper tape.

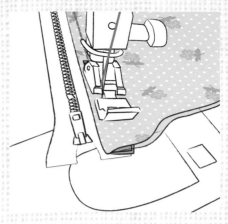

3 Fold back the top edge of all three layers (the lining, the printed fabric and the zip) by about ⅜in (10mm). Then topstitch on the right side, close to the fold.

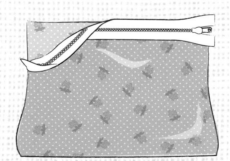

4 Fold the fabric in half, with the right sides together, to align the edges of the fabric with the other edge of the zipper tape. Pin, baste and machine stitch.

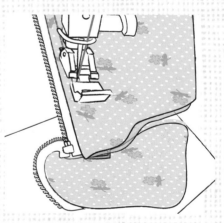

5 You now have a tube of fabric joined with a zipper. Open the zipper and topstitch the second side.

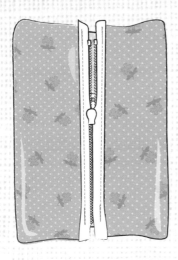

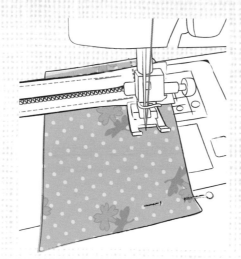

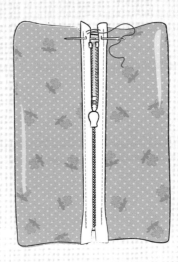

6 Do the zipper up about halfway. Turn the bag wrong side out and flatten the tube with the zipper in the centre, as shown.

7 Pin and stitch the seam across the end where the zipper is closed, ⅝in (15mm) from the edges.

8 Do the same at the other end but, before stitching, baste the ends of the zipper tape together.

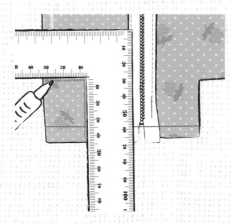

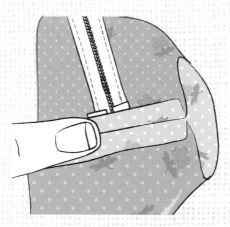

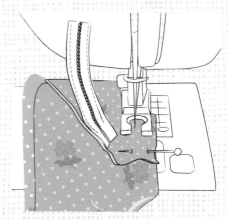

9 Measure and mark a rectangle 1¾in x 1¼ in (4.5 x 3cm) on each corner. Take the smaller measurement from the folded edge and the larger measurement from the seamed end. Cut along the lines.

10 Open out each corner and flatten, so that the end of the seam is in the centre.

11 Press the seam to one side, away from the zip. Stitch each corner seam, then turn the bag right sides out through the opening in the zipper.

ZIGZAG STITCHED APPLIQUÉ

A CLOSE ZIGZAG STITCH, WITH THE STITCH-LENGTH DIAL SET TO JUST ABOVE ZERO, RESEMBLES SATIN STITCH AND IS PERFECT FOR CREATING APPLIQUÉ. PRACTISE ZIGZAG STITCHES ON SPARE FABRIC, EXPERIMENTING WITH THE STITCH LENGTH.

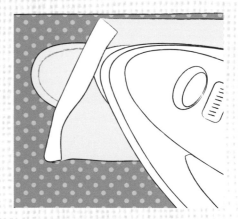

The zigzag stitch is one of the main features of modern sewing machines, where the needle is able to swing from side to side, allowing you to stitch not only straight seams but a range of other stitches, including buttonholes.

Appliqué – applying fabric shapes to a background fabric – is an easy and effective way to add decorative detail and to personalize your sewing projects. Fusible bonding web – a special adhesive material applied to fabric using a hot iron – makes machine appliqué quick to do and fairly foolproof.

1 Draw your motif on the backing paper of the bonding web, making sure the design is reversed. Cut out roughly, leaving a small margin of about ⅛in (3mm) all round.

2 Place the cutout, adhesive side down, on the wrong side of the fabric and press using a hot iron without steam. Place a piece of spare fabric or kitchen towel on top first, to protect the baseplate of the iron.

Tip A stitch length setting from between 1 and 5 will give you an open zigzag stitch, while for a closed stitch – satin stitch – you will need to set the dial between 0 and 1. You can set the stitch width to any size you like: try out the stitch on a spare piece of fabric so that you know which setting works best for you, making sure that the stitch is wide enough to cover the edge of the fabric.

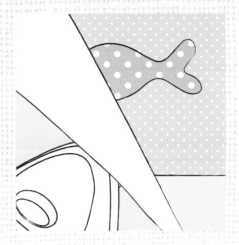

3 Cut out neatly around the drawn lines. Peel off the backing paper to reveal the adhesive.

4 Place the cutout shape, adhesive side down, on the right side of the background fabric.

5 Press, using a hot iron. Once again, it is a good idea to use a piece of kitchen paper or scrap fabric to protect your iron. The motif is now ready to stitch.

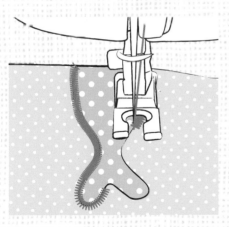

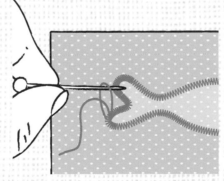

6 Set the machine to your chosen stitch length and width, place the fabric under the needle, drop the lever and manually lower the needle into the fabric. Stitch around the edge of the motif, making sure the stitches cover the cut edge neatly.

7 Cut the threads. For a neat finish, turn over the work and pull the top thread end through to the wrong side – lift up the thread tail, stick a pin through the loop of the stitch before it and pull it out. Knot the threads together.

Project seven

TABLET COVER

PRACTISE YOUR ZIGZAG STITCHES ON THIS PRACTICAL AND RATHER STYLISH COVER.
CONSTRUCTED LIKE AN ENVELOPE, WITH A FLAP AT ONE END THAT CAN BE TUCKED IN,
THE COVER IS MADE FROM COTTON FABRICS WITH A LAYER OF WADDING INSIDE.

YOU WILL NEED

- Printed cotton fabric, approximately 25 x 8½in (64 x 22cm)
- Plain or printed cotton fabric, approximately 25 x 8½in (64 x 22cm), for lining
- Cotton batting (wadding) or thermal curtain interlining, approximately 25 x 8½in (64 x 22cm)
- Fusible bonding web
- Ruler
- Pencil
- Small pieces of cotton and linen fabric, in a range of different colours and patterns, for the appliqué
- Sewing thread to match fabric

FINISHED SIZE

With the top flap folded over, the cover size is 10 x 6¾in (25.5 x 17.5cm)

TECHNIQUES USED

Straight stitch and zigzag stitch (see page 32)
Hems (see page 40)
Seams (see page 48)
Zigzag stitched appliqué (see page 78)

MATERIALS TO USE

A layer of wadding inside the cover will help to cushion your precious tablet and protect it from bumps and scratches when you're on the go. Choose washable fabrics and pre-shrink them before cutting and stitching.

Tip These measurements fit a popular brand of tablet. To check that they fit your tablet, place it on the fabric and allow 1in (25mm) all round. Pin and baste before machine-stitching, to double-check that it fits.

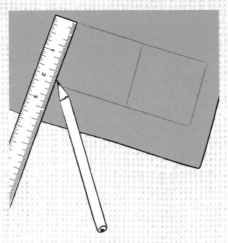

1. Cut the main fabric, lining and wadding to 25¼ x 8⅝in (64 x 22cm), or to fit your tablet (see page 80).

2. Using a ruler and pencil, draw one 4in (10cm) square and four 2in (5cm) squares on the backing paper of the bonding web. Cut out, following the lines you have drawn, then place each one on a different scrap of fabric and bond in place using a hot iron.

3. Cut out, with a margin of ³⁄₁₆in (5mm) around the edge of the bonding web, then pull several rows of threads out all round, to create a fringed edge.

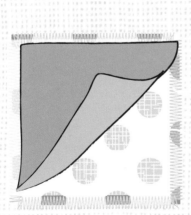

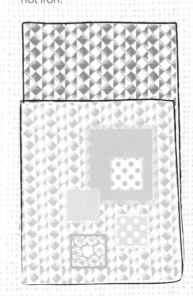

4. Peel off the backing paper from each piece.

5. Fold the main fabric so that there is 3½in (9cm) at the top (which will be the flap), then arrange the fabric squares on the front of the cover, clear of side seam allowances and at least ¾in (2cm) up from the fold at the base.

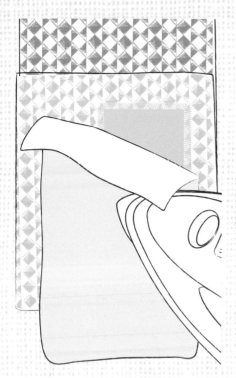
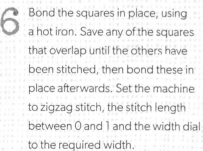
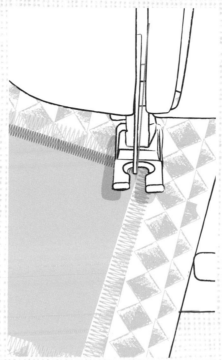
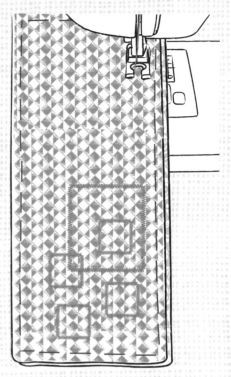

6 Bond the squares in place, using a hot iron. Save any of the squares that overlap until the others have been stitched, then bond these in place afterwards. Set the machine to zigzag stitch, the stitch length between 0 and 1 and the width dial to the required width.

7 Zigzag stitch all round each square, ³⁄₁₆in (5mm) from the edge; in other words, just inside the fringed edge. Each time you come to a corner, lower the needle into the fabric, lift the presser foot, turn the work by 90°, lower the foot and continue stitching. Press the work on the wrong side.

8 Place the main fabric and lining right sides together and pin, then baste. Starting at the end with the appliqué (the front of the case), stitch a ³⁄₈in (1cm) seam down one long edge, across the short edge and up the other long edge. Fasten off securely. Clip the corners using a diagonal cut (see page 39) and turn right sides out. Press.

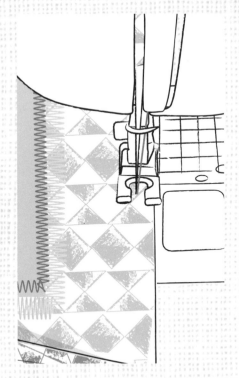

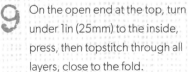

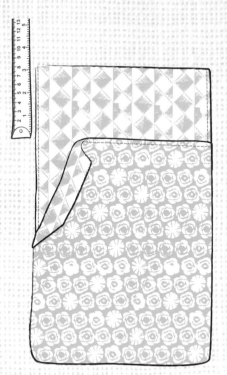

9 On the open end at the top, turn under 1in (25mm) to the inside, press, then topstitch through all layers, close to the fold.

10 Fold the cover so that the lining is on the outside and bring the topstitched edge up to 3¼in (8cm) below the top edge. Pin the sides (and baste if you wish), then stitch down both sides, through all the layers, ¼in (6mm) from the edges. Be sure to backstitch at both ends of these two seams.

11 Turn the cover right sides out and push out the bottom corners with a blunt object, such as a chopstick. Place the tablet inside the cover and tuck in the flap.

GATHERS, PLEATS AND TUCKS

THESE ARE METHODS USED TO DISTRIBUTE FULLNESS IN FABRIC, SUCH AS WHEN YOU ARE MAKING CURTAINS OR A FULL SKIRT. GATHERS ARE FAIRLY UNSTRUCTURED, WHILE PLEATS AND TUCKS ARE MORE UNIFORM AND REQUIRE ACCURATE MEASURING.

GATHERING

Gathering is usually worked on the edge of a piece of fabric that is to be joined to an ungathered piece. This is the method most commonly used to create frills.

PLEATS

There are three main types of pleats: knife pleats, box pleats and inverted pleats. Knife pleats are usually used on garments, such as pleated skirts. Box pleats – the kind of pleat you often find on the back of a man's shirt – can be used for curtain headings. While a box pleat sits on the surface of the fabric, an inverted pleat, as the name suggests, is like a reversed box pleat and is often used on pelmets, bed valances and loose chair covers.

On crisp fabrics, pleats are usually pressed to give a crisp crease, while pleats on soft fabrics are usually left unpressed.

Below left: gathering
Below right: pleats

TUCKS

Tucks are stitched folds, made on the right side of the fabric and following the straight grain. They can be made in different widths, the narrowest of which are known as pintucks.

To make pintucks, you need to make a series of neat creases in the fabric, then stitch close to the fold to hold the crease in place. Pintucks are usually grouped in parallel lines and they look very effective on clothing – in vertical lines on a shirt front, for example, or horizontal lines above the hem of a skirt – or on bedlinen and cushions.

The pleats and tucks shown in the step-by-step instructions are 1in (25mm) wide but they can be any width you like. Make a few samples on spare pieces of fabric, to experiment with different widths, to create various different effects.

Tip Pintucks can be used to shorten hems and sleeves. So, for example, if you are making a child's dress, you could add a few rows of pintucks above the hemline; these could then be unpicked later, and the crease ironed out, to make the garment longer.

HOW TO GATHER FABRIC

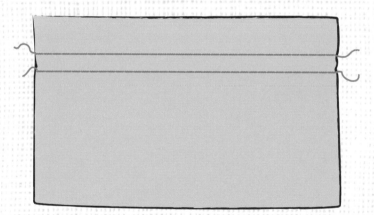

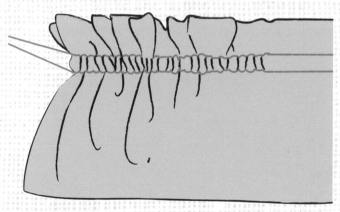

1 Stitch a line of straight stitch close to the top of the edge to be gathered. Use a long machine stitch. Sew a second line of stitches parallel to the first.

2 Make sure one end of each row of stitches is secure, then hold the two bobbin threads at the other end, and pull to gather the fabric.

MAKING KNIFE PLEATS

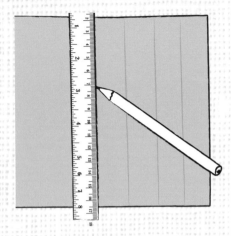

1 Mark lines 1in (25mm) apart on the right side of the fabric, with an erasable pen or tailor's chalk, to show the positions of the pleats. To make each pleat you need to draw two fold lines: one for the fold and one to indicate the placement.

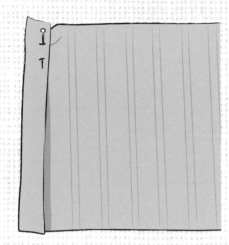

2 Fold the fabric along the first line then fold it over on to the placement line. Pin to hold it in place.

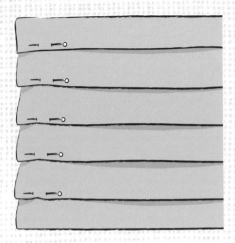

3 Continue folding and pinning until all the pleats are in place. The folds face in the same direction.

4 Press the pleats, removing the pins as you go, to create sharp creases.

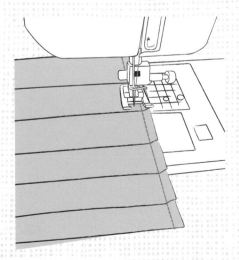

5 Stitch along the top edge of the pleats, to hold them in place. Sew a second line of stitching to make sure the pleats are held securely in place.

MAKING PARALLEL PINTUCKS

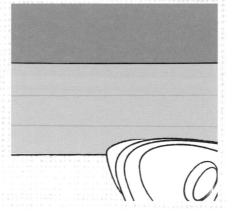

1 Use a ruler and an erasable marker pen, or tailor's chalk, to mark parallel lines 1in (25mm) apart on the fabric.

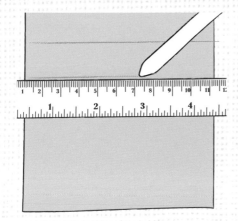

2 Fold the fabric along each of these lines in turn, and press to create a crisp crease.

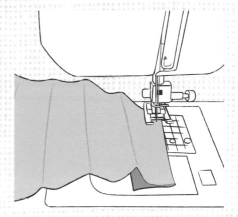

3 Machine stitch each of the tucks, sewing close to the folded edge.

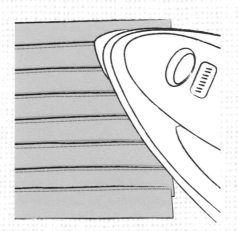

4 When all the tucks have been stitched, press with a warm iron, pushing the tucks to one side so that they all lie flat.

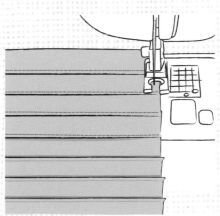

5 Machine a line of stitching along the ends of the tucks, on both ends, to hold them in place.

CUSHION COVER

PINTUCKING PRODUCES A LOVELY RIDGED TEXTURE, WHICH IS IDEAL FOR HOME FURNISHINGS. THIS CUSHION COVER WOULD SUIT ANY INTERIOR. A SPOT-PRINTED FABRIC HAS BEEN USED HERE, BUT YOU CAN CHOOSE YOUR OWN TO MATCH YOUR DECOR.

YOU WILL NEED

- 16in (40cm) of spot-print cotton fabric, 44in (112cm) wide
- Sewing thread to match fabric
- 15in (38cm) cushion pad

FINISHED SIZE

Finished cushion measures 15in (38cm) square.

TECHNIQUES USED

Straight stitch (see page 32)
Hems (see page 40)
Seams (see page 48)

MATERIALS TO USE

Spot-print fabric is a good choice for this project, as you can follow the rows of spots to mark and stitch regularly spaced lines. A woven check or stripe would also be a good choice of fabric. This project shows that you can make a stylish cushion cover quite economically. The pieces are cut from a 16in (40cm) length of fabric. Choose a fabric that is 44in (112cm) wide and trim off the selvedges. Measurements given in the project are based on the piece of fabric measuring 42½ x 16in (108 x 40cm) once the selvedges have been trimmed off.

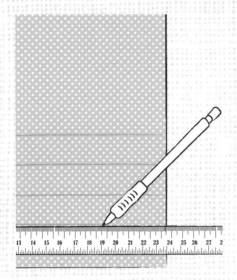

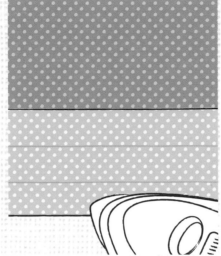

1 Trim off the selvedges, then cut the fabric into two pieces, each measuring approximately 21 x 16in (54 x 40cm). Mark a line across the centre of the whole width on one piece of fabric, then measure 1in (25mm) to one side of this line and draw a second line, parallel to the first. Draw more parallel lines, 1in (25mm) apart, until you reach the edge, then draw a further set of lines at 1in (25mm) intervals on the other side of the centre line.

2 Fold along the line at one end, with wrong sides together, and press to form a sharp crease. Repeat, in turn, with all the other lines, taking care not to flatten previous creases.

3 Stitch along the first tuck, ⅛in (1–2mm) from the fold. Stitch along the remaining folds in the same way.

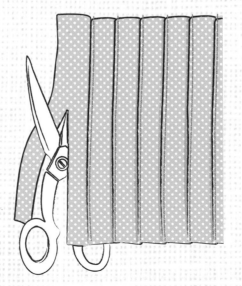

4 Once all the pintucks have been stitched, press to one side, then lay the fabric flat on the work surface and measure the width. If necessary, trim the fabric so that you have a 15¾in (40cm) square.

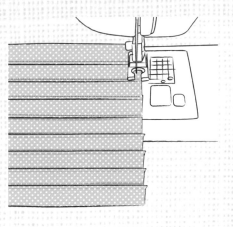

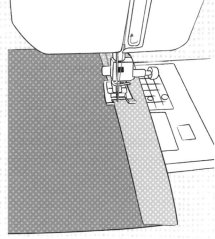

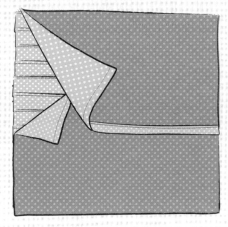

5 Stitch along the ends of the pintucks, about ⅜in (1cm) from the raw edge.

6 Cut the remaining piece of fabric in half: you should have two pieces, each measuring 15¾in x 10⅝ in (40 x 27cm). Hem one long edge on each piece of fabric by turning it under by ⅜in (1cm) then again by ⅝in (1.5cm). Stitch.

7 Place the pintucked piece (cushion front) right side up on the work surface. Place one of the hemmed pieces on top, lining up the raw edges, with the hem towards the centre. Place the second hemmed piece on top, so that the hemmed edges overlap. Pin and baste all round, then remove the pins. Machine stitch all round with a ⅜in (10mm) seam allowance.

8 Remove the basting. Clip corners and turn right sides out, press, and insert the cushion pad.

Tip Leave the back opening as it is, or add press fasteners or pieces of Velcro to fasten, if you wish.

MACHINE EMBROIDERY

A MODERN ELECTRIC SEWING MACHINE WITH A FOOT PEDAL LEAVES BOTH YOUR HANDS FREE SO THAT YOU CAN MANIPULATE THE FABRIC AS YOU STITCH. THIS ALLOWS YOU TO BE MORE CREATIVE WITH YOUR STITCHING AND WORK SOME FREESTYLE EMBROIDERY TECHNIQUES.

Usually when you are machine stitching, the feed dogs, next to the needle plate, feed the fabric through with each up-and-down movement of the needle. When free-stitching with a sewing machine – for machine embroidery or for darning – you need to be able to move the fabric in different directions as you stitch, so the feed dogs have to be disengaged. Check your machine's manual for instructions on how to do this.

An open-toe presser foot has a transparent plastic section that allows you to see the fabric more clearly so that you can see stitches in progress.

You can stitch using a straight stitch or a zigzag. Try both to see which you find easier. For either stitch, set the stitch length to zero; for zigzag stitch, try different widths: a narrow width setting of between 1 and 3 is best when you are learning the technique.

NEEDLES

For machine embroidery, a thicker needle is needed, such as a 16/100. You can buy special needles designed for machine embroidery. In order to decide which size needle size best suits your machine and your choice of fabric and threads, practise first on a spare piece of fabric.

THREADS

Ordinary sewing thread can be used to try out machine embroidery techniques; once you are confident, you can use special machine embroidery threads, which are stronger, easier to use and less liable to tangle and fray. These are slightly more expensive and are available in a range of attractive colours and finishes, including cotton and polyester threads, in matt or glossy finishes, plain, variegated and even fluorescent colours; rayon threads, which have a silky sheen; and metallic threads in gold, silver and glittery colours.

FABRICS

Machine embroidery, especially when it is applied very densely, can distort the fabric. As a general rule, you should work with the fabric stretched in a hoop. Some fabrics are easier to work with than others: a firm, closely woven cotton or linen is the best choice while you are learning; velvet, silks and sheer fabrics are more challenging and often need some kind of backing or support, so save these until you become more experienced in the technique.

EMBROIDERY HOOP

You can use any embroidery hoop to keep your fabric taut, which is important when machine embroidering as the stitches might otherwise cause the fabric to pucker and distort. A spring clip hoop is shown below.

To use an embroidery hoop, separate the rings and place your fabric over the inner ring. Press the outer ring down around the inner ring: if you are using the spring clip version you will have to pinch the clips together to open out the outer hoop, and if you are using the screw version you may have to loosen the screw.

There should be fabric overlapping around all sides of the hoop. Release the spring clip or tighten the screw to keep the fabric in place, and you are ready to stitch. Make sure you place the hoop under the machine needle so that the fabric is flat on the base plate.

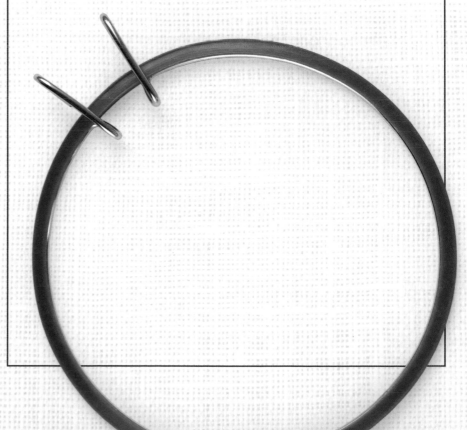

HOW TO STITCH A MACHINE EMBROIDERY DESIGN

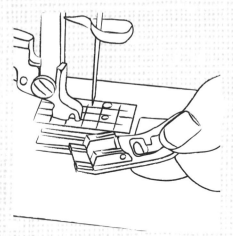

1 Remove the presser foot and lower the feed dogs. Check your machine's manual to see how to do this.

2 Draw your design on to the fabric using an erasable marker.

3 Stretch the fabric in an embroidery hoop. The design you have drawn should be inside the hoop so that the wrong side lies flat on the sewing machine.

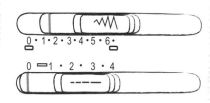

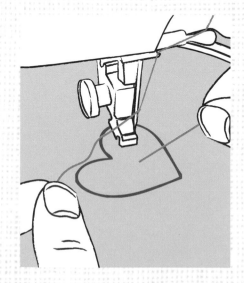

4 Place the fabric flat on the bed of the machine. Lower the drop feed lever. Set the stitch length to zero and select a straight or zigzag stitch; if you choose zigzag, select the width as well.

5 Turn the hand wheel so that the needle goes into the fabric at the starting point. Lift the needle by turning the wheel again, and draw the lower (bobbin) thread through to the surface of the fabric.

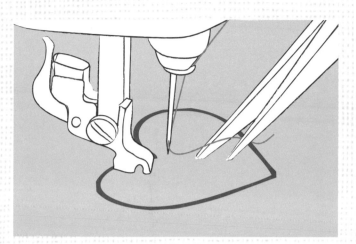
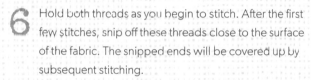
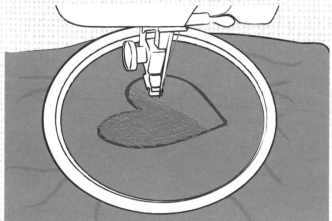

6 Hold both threads as you begin to stitch. After the first few stitches, snip off these threads close to the surface of the fabric. The snipped ends will be covered up by subsequent stitching.

7 As you stitch, use your fingertips on the edges of the hoop to guide the fabric back and forth and from side to side. Continue stitching until the whole area has been filled with a thick layer of overlapping stitches, then raise the needle and snip off the threads.

MACHINE EMBROIDERY TIPS

- Make sure you keep the fabric flat on the bed of the sewing machine.

- Do not tilt the embroidery hoop but move it backwards and forwards, and from side to side.

- Depress the foot pedal slowly and steadily, so that the needle does not move too quickly; this makes it easier to control while stitching.

- If you find it difficult to embroider using straight stitch, try zigzag instead – or vice versa.

- Use the same thread in the bobbin and on the spool; threads of different types or thicknesses can cause tangling to occur.

- If the thread gets tangled, stop immediately, remove the hoop and fabric from the machine and deal with the problem, re-threading the bobbin and the needle where necessary.

EMBROIDERED PICTURE

PRACTISE YOUR NEW MACHINE EMBROIDERY STITCHING SKILLS ON THIS LITTLE PICTURE THEN FRAME YOUR HANDIWORK. ONCE YOU HAVE MASTERED THE TECHNIQUE IT IS EASY TO DRAW YOUR OWN DESIGNS, OR TRACE THEM FROM VARIOUS SOURCES.

YOU WILL NEED
- Plain cotton fabric in white or a light colour, approximately 10in (25cm) square
- Template (see right)
- Erasable marking pen
- Embroidery hoop, 8in (20cm) diameter
- Machine embroidery thread in brown, green, blue, violet and orange
- Hand-sewing needle
- Frame with 4¾in (12cm) square aperture

FINISHED SIZE
Embroidered area is approximately 4¾in (12cm) square

TECHNIQUES USED
Machine embroidery (see page 94)

MATERIALS TO USE
Use a firm fabric as this is less likely to distort when you stretch it in a frame. Machine embroidery thread is easier to work with for this technique than ordinary sewing thread.

TEMPLATE (COPY AT 100%)

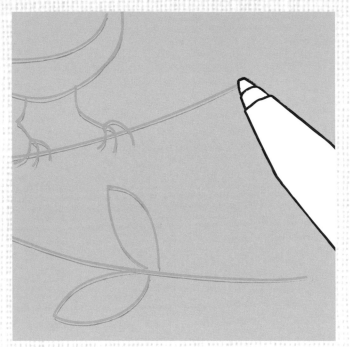

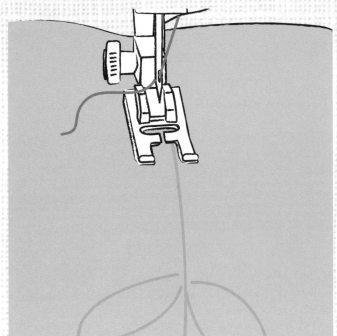

1 Place the fabric centrally on top of the design and trace the lines, using an erasable marking pen. By using a light-coloured fabric, you should be able to see the lines easily through the fabric.

2 Place the fabric under the needle at the end of the lower branch, on the right-hand side.

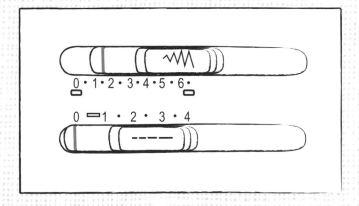

3 Set the stitch length to zero and set the width dial to the desired width. Wind the bobbin with brown thread and put a reel of brown thread on the spool pin.

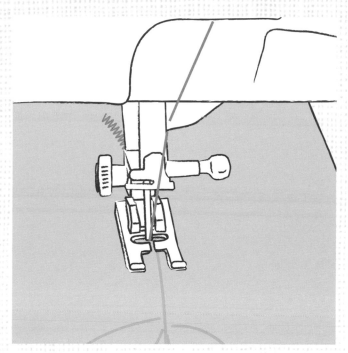

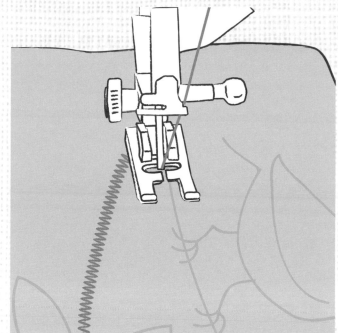

4 Lower the pressure foot. Turn the hand wheel so that the needle goes into the fabric at the starting point, then start stitching along the line you have drawn.

5 When you reach the end of the branch, lower the needle into the fabric, raise the presser foot and swivel the fabric, ready to stitch the second branch. Lower the presser foot and resume stitching, once again following the line you have drawn. Then, with the same thread and stitch settings, embroider the outline of the bird's breast and the legs.

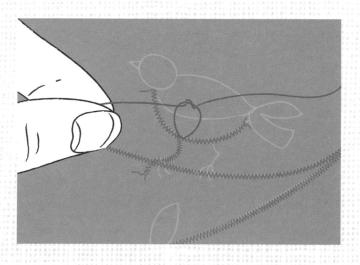

6 As you finish each line of stitching, do not backstitch but cut the threads, leaving ends about 2–2⅜in (5–6cm) long. On the wrong side, pull the lower thread so that the upper thread comes through, then knot the two threads together.

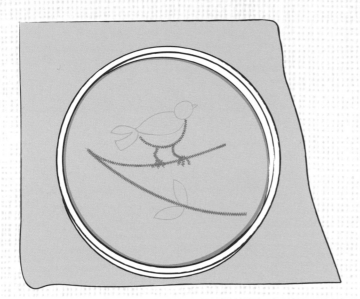

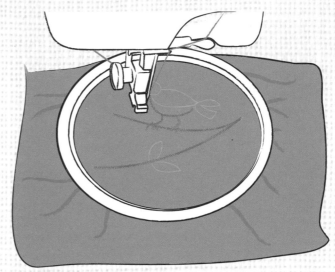

7 Stretch the fabric in an embroidery hoop. The design should be right side up inside the hoop so that the wrong side lies flat on the machine. Replace bobbin and spool threads with green thread.

8 Remove the presser foot and lower the feed dogs. Place the hoop flat on the bed of the machine. Set the stitch length to zero and select a straight or zigzag stitch. Set the width dial to the desired width.

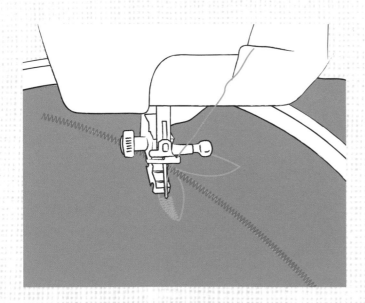

9 Lower the drop feed lever and turn the hand wheel so that the needle goes into the fabric at the starting point, in the centre of one of the leaves. Lift the needle by turning the wheel again, and draw the lower (bobbin) thread through to the surface of the fabric. Hold both threads as you begin to stitch. After the first few stitches, snip off these threads close to the surface of the fabric. Continue stitching until both leaves have been filled.

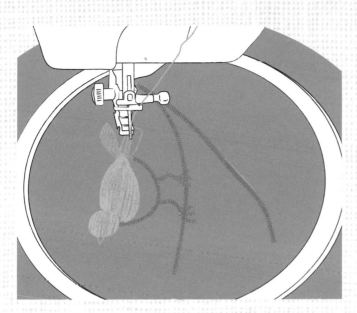

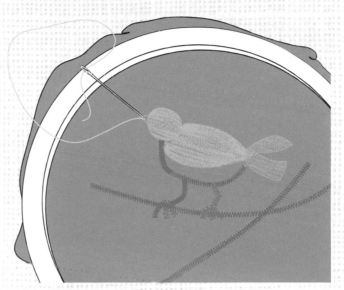

10 Replace bobbin and spool threads with blue and fill in the bird's wing and head. Change to violet thread and fill in the tail feathers.

11 You might find it difficult to machine embroider small areas such as the bird's beak, so remove the work from the machine, thread a hand-sewing needle with orange thread and fill in the area by hand, stitching a series of small overlapping stitches to mimic the machine embroidery. Finally, stitch a bead in place for the bird's eye.

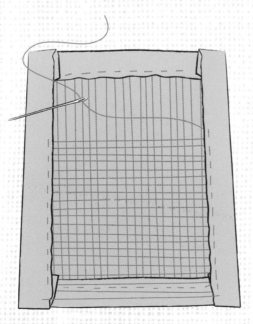

12 To frame the sampler, cut a piece of card to fit inside your chosen frame and place it on the centre back of the embroidery. Trim the fabric to give a border of 2–2⅜in (5–6cm) all round, then fold it over the edges of the card. You can glue it to the card or, to be more traditional, lace the edges of the fabric together with thread. Remove the glass from the frame, place the embroidery inside, and replace the backing board.

Resources

Fabrics
The Cotton Patch
1283–1285 Stratford Road
Hall Green
Birmingham
B28 9AJ
+44 (0)121 702 2840
www.cottonpatch.co.uk

Fabrics and books on sewing
Laughing Hens
www.laughinghens.com

Haberdashery and craft supplies
Sewing Online
9 Mallard Road
Victoria Business Park
Netherfield
Nottingham
NG4 2PE
+44 (0)115 9874422
www.sewing-online.com

Haberdashery, fabrics and sewing classes
for all skill levels
Ray-Stitch
99 Essex Road
London
N1 2SJ
+44 (0)207 704 1060
www.raystitch.co.uk

Online sewing tutorials
Craftsy
www.craftsy.com

Crafty Gemini
www.craftygemini.blogspot.co.uk

Professor Pincushion
www.professorpincushion.com

Sewing, quilting and embroidery threads
Mettler
Amann Handel GmbH
89165 Dietenheim
Germany
www.amann-mettler.com

Sewing accessories, haberdashery
and paper patterns
Sew Direct
+44 (0) 884 880 1263
www.sewdirect.com

Sewing supplies
Morplan
Unit 1
Temple Bank
Harlow
Essex
CM20 2DY
0800 451122 (UK only)
www.morplan.com

Glossary

backing
A second layer of fabric placed behind a main fabric, with or without a layer of wadding or interlining in between.

baste
To sew pieces of fabric together temporarily, using a long, loose line of stitches. Also known as tacking.

bias cut
A cut made on the diagonal, across the fabric's lengthwise and crosswise grain. A cut made across the bias (diagonal) of a woven fabric is less likely to fray.

fray
A cut made across the lengthwise or crosswise grain of a fabric exposes thread ends that are then prone to unravel, or fray.

gathering
The technique of sewing a line of stitches then pulling up the thread so that the fabric is formed into folds or pleats.

grain
The arrangement of threads in a woven fabric, where weft (crosswise) threads are woven back and forth between warp (lengthwise) threads.

hem
A method of turning under and stitching the cut edge of a piece of fabric to neaten it and prevent fraying.

motif
A decorative shape that can be cut from fabric or embroidered, for example.

neaten
This applies to a method used to turn under or otherwise finish off a raw edge.

non-woven fabric
A material with fibres bonded together by chemical, mechanical or heat treatment – such as interfacings, wadding and felt.

pattern
Refers both to the design printed or woven into a fabric, and a paper template used as a guide to cutting fabric pieces.

raw edge
The cut edge of fabric, without a selvedge or hem.

right side
The fabric surface that will show on the outside of the finished project. On most plain fabrics or those with woven stripes or checks, either side can be the right side.

seam
A line of stitching that joins two pieces of fabric together.

seam allowance
The area between the raw (cut) edge of the fabric and the seamline. The most common seam allowances are ¼in, ½in and ⅝in (6mm, 12mm and 15mm).

seamline
The line along which you stitch a seam.

selvedge
The finished edge on either side of a piece of fabric, which will not fray or unravel.

snip
To make a small cut in fabric, usually with the tips of a pair of scissors.

tail
The end of a length of thread.

template
A shape that can be cut from a material such as paper, card or plastic and used as a guide for cutting fabric.

wrong side
The surface of the fabric that will be on the inside of a finished project.

About the author

Artist, writer and designer Susie Johns grew up in a household where drawing and making things were very much encouraged – both her parents and all four grandparents were creative people.

Having studied Fine Art at the Slade School, London, Susie began her publishing career as a magazine and partworks editor before becoming a freelance writer and designer. She is the author of more than 30 craft books – including *Knitted Finger Puppets*, *Knitted Pets* and *Knitted Woodland Creatures* – on a range of subjects including knitting, crochet, papier mâché and embroidery. Susie has also contributed to a number of magazines, such as *Let's Knit*, *Crafts Beautiful*, *Embroidery* and *Needlecraft*. She particularly enjoys art and craft activities that involve recycling and reinventing.

Susie is a qualified teacher and runs workshops in drawing and painting, knitting and crochet, embroidery and 3D design near her home in Greenwich, London.

Acknowledgements

AUTHOR'S ACKNOWLEDGEMENTS
Many thanks to the following for their help in creating this book: Jonathan Bailey, for asking me to do it in the first place; Andrew Perris and Rebecca Mothersole for the attractive photography and styling, and for making sure the finished book looks so inviting; Sarah Skeate for her skilful illustrations; and last, but by no means least, Sara Harper for her support and her patience under pressure.

GMC PUBLICATIONS WOULD LIKE TO THANK THE FOLLOWING PEOPLE: The Old Forge, South Heighton, East Sussex, for allowing us to shoot on location in their house and garden, Emma Foster for her help with photographic styling.

Index

To order a book, or to request
a catalogue, contact:

GMC Publications Ltd
Castle Place, 166 High Street,
Lewes, East Sussex,
BN7 1XU
United Kingdom
Tel: +44 (0)1273 488005
www.gmcbooks.com